Diet recommendations for fructose malabsorption

Please check these recommendations always with a nutrition consultant, therapist, doctor or dietician. The recipes and the list of ingredients are supporting the conventional medical therapy.
The calorie disclosures of fresh ingredients (fruit and vegetables) vary according to quality and time of harvest. The contents were checked by a dietician and a nutrition consultant for the Traditional Chinese Medicine (TCM).

Author:
©2017 Josef Miligui
www.ebns.at

AF236918

Source:
The lists are created from the EBNS database for nutritional counseling. The database is used by dietitians, therapists and doctors for advising the patient / client.

Literature:
The specialist literature and the training documents of the German and Austrian dietary and traditional Chinese medicine serve as a knowledge base. We have used the documents as a basis of knowledge, adapted it to our experience and completed them.
http://di-book.com

Title Photo:
©2008 Erika Weixlbaumer

Production and publishing:
BoD – Books on Demand, Norderstedt
ISBN: 9783752869514

Diet recommendations for DIETETICS - Gastrointestinal tract - Small intestine and large intestine - Fructose malabsorption

1 Treatment strategy..5
2 Avoid 6
3 Breakfast 6
4 Snack 7
5 Lunch 7
6 Afternoon...9
7 Dinner...9
8 Any time 11
9 Recipes 12
   9.1   Adzuki Bean and Rice Soup................................12
   9.2   Andalusian fish pot..12
   9.3   Antipasti...13
   9.4   Asparagus Cream Soup 14
   9.5   Barley and vegetable soup 15
   9.6   Barley soup..16
   9.7   Basic recipe for a beef broth (clear)..................16
   9.8   Basic recipe for a chicken broth worming..........17
   9.9   Basic recipe for a duck broth 18
   9.10   Basic recipe for a fish broth...........................18
   9.11   Basic recipe for a reissue soup (Congee).........19
   9.12   Basic recipe for a vegetable soup, nutritious ...20
   9.13   Bean paste piquant sweet...............................21
   9.14   Beef pumpkin and vegetable stew..................21
   9.15   Beef salad 22
   9.16   Beluga lentil stew with vegetables..................23
   9.17   Black beans with avocado...............................24
   9.18   Black root with yogurt.....................................25
   9.19   Boiled fillet with potato (Austrian classic Tafelspitz)...........25
   9.20   Broccoli cream soup 26
   9.21   Bulgur with tomatoes and fresh herbs 27
   9.22   Carp soup..28
   9.23   Carrot and potato rucola sandwich..................29
   9.24   Carrot Risotto 30
   9.25   Champignon rice 30
   9.26   Champignon salad with cress 31
   9.27   Chicken in an ilalian style................................32
   9.28   Chicken soup with green spelt, parsley and sake 33
   9.29   Chicken with white turnips on rice 34

9.30	Classic ginger chicken with rice wine	35
9.31	Cod soup with tomatoes	36
9.32	Colorful tuscan bean soup	36
9.33	Corn coffee with cardamom	37
9.34	Couscous Salad	37
9.35	Cream cheese substitute	38
9.36	Dal - spicy lentils	39
9.37	Delicately spiced zucchini with tomatoes	40
9.38	Fennel and potato gratin	41
9.39	Fennel with roasted walnuts	42
9.40	Fennel-Rice Soup	42
9.41	Fine Russian borscht	43
9.42	Fish soup with rosemary	44
9.43	Grilled lamb chops with sweet potato puree & vegetables	45
9.44	Grilled salmon steaks with cauliflower and potatoes	46
9.45	Grilled tomatoes with cheese filling	47
9.46	Hearty polenta mash	48
9.47	Hearty winter breakfast	48
9.48	Hungarian rice salad	49
9.49	Italian champignon rice	50
9.50	Kohlrabi in chervil sauce with potatoes	51
9.51	Lasagne with tofu cream	52
9.52	Legumes	52
9.53	Lettuce with fresh cheese	53
9.54	Lettuce with vinegar dressing	54
9.55	Marinated cod on pumpkin puree	55
9.56	Millet with egg and butter	56
9.57	Miso soup with tofu	56
9.58	Oat Congee	57
9.59	Oatmeal soup with spring onion and carrots	57
9.60	Oven potatoes with celery-curd cheese (quark)	58
9.61	Pancakes with spinach and parmesan	59
9.62	Paprika turkey with rice and lettuce	60
9.63	Polenta with ratatouille	61
9.64	Potato bags with wild herbs and tomato sauce	62
9.65	Potato cream with herbs and fresh cheese	63
9.66	Potato gnocchi with vegetables and basil sauce	64
9.67	Potato pancakes	65
9.68	Potato-basil soup	66
9.69	Potatoes with wild garlic-curd cheese	66
9.70	Quick zucchini soup	67
9.71	Refreshing cucumber soup with potatoes	68
9.72	Ribbon noodles with leaf spinach	68

9.73	Rice congee with chicken liver and buckthorn fruit	69
9.74	Rice pesto with pine nuts	70
9.75	Roasted barley patties	70
9.76	Roasted millet with Celery sticks	72
9.77	Rosemary Potatoes	72
9.78	Russian kasha with white cabbage	73
9.79	Salmon on tomato-spinach	73
9.80	Semolina soup with vegetables	74
9.81	Sliced lamb with rosemary potatoes	75
9.82	Spinach with Tahini	76
9.83	Spring salad	77
9.84	Stew with sweet potato and leeks	77
9.85	Sweet potato pancakes with basil pesto	78
9.86	Tea from basil	79
9.87	Tea from chamomile	79
9.88	Tea from lime blossom	80
9.89	Tea from mallow	80
9.90	Tea Green tea	81
9.91	Tofu-Black Bean Chili with Rice	81
9.92	Turkey breast with vegetables (Asian)	82
9.93	Vegetable bowl with tofu and curry on rice	83
9.94	Vegetable miso soup with tofu	84
9.95	Vegetable rice	85
9.96	Yellow lentil soup	86
9.97	Zucchini with basil pesto	87
10	Effects of food	88
10.1	Use ingredients: recommendable	88
10.2	Use ingredients: yes	89
10.3	Use ingredients: little	94
10.4	Do not use contra-acting foods	95
11	Herbs and their effects	96
11.1	Basil	96
11.2	Mugwort	96
11.3	Savory	96
11.4	Nettles	96
11.5	Dill	96
11.6	Chamomile	96
11.7	Chervil dried	96
11.8	Coriander	97
11.9	Coriander (fresh)	97
11.10	Herbs various	97
11.11	Cress	97
11.12	Chives	97

11.13	Lovage	97
11.14	Lily bulbs	97
11.15	Dandelion (young plants)	97
11.16	Marjoram	98
11.17	Oregano fresh	98
11.18	Oregano dried	98
11.19	Parsley	98
11.20	Peppermint	98
11.21	Rosemary	98
11.22	Sage	98
11.23	Sorrel	98
11.24	Black caraway	99
11.25	Thyme dried	99
11.26	King Solomon's-seal	99
11.27	Yam root, yam root tuber	99
12	Basics of Nutrition	100
12.1	Nutrition	100
12.2	Recipes	102
12.3	Foodstuffs	102
12.4	Herbs	103
13	Other dietic-books	104

1 Treatment strategy

Avoiding fruit sugar containing food, e.g. certain fruit varieties with high proportion of fruit sugar, fruit juices.
Avoid sorbitol, because the fruit sugar resorption is thereby blocked.
Avoid lactose-containing foods, because milk sugar tolerance often occurs together with the disease.
General recommendations:
Only eat after a rich meal.
Slowly consume foods with fruit content, e.g. Juice dilute or take small sips. Avoiding ready-to-use meals which can be used to prepare milk sugar powders as carriers or with fruit sugar substitutes (sorbitol, isomalt, mannitol, xylitol, etc.).
Wholesome preparation of the dishes such as stewing, steaming, prefer.
Avoiding grilling, deep-frying, frying.
Season with a lot of herbs.
Eat fruit sugar together with grapes sugar to improve the intake of the fruit sugar.
Sufficient fluid intake, 1.5-2 liters per day.

2 Avoid

Incompatible fruits as well as foodstuffs produced from them such as fruit juices, compotes, etc.
Honey, Diabetic Products, Some Sweets.

3 Breakfast

kkal. per serving

Adzuki Bean and Rice Soup 199
Barley and vegetable soup 281
Barley soup 265
Basic recipe for a beef broth (clear) 114
Basic recipe for a chicken broth worming 89
Basic recipe for a duck broth 61
Basic recipe for a reissue soup (Congee) 140
Basic recipe for a vegetable soup, nutritious 47
Bean paste piquant sweet 311
Beef salad 249
Black beans with avocado 263
Bulgur with tomatoes and fresh herbs 205
Carrot and potato rucola sandwich 94
Carrot Risotto 308
Champignon rice 410
Colorful tuscan bean soup 249
Corn coffee with cardamom 3
Couscous Salad 338
Cream cheese substitute 526
Delicately spiced zucchini with tomatoes 203
Fennel-Rice Soup 155
Fish soup with rosemary 271
Hearty polenta mash 262
Hearty winter breakfast 678
Hungarian rice salad 421
Italian champignon rice 256
Kohlrabi in chervil sauce with potatoes 187
Legumes 31
Lettuce with vinegar dressing 67
Millet with egg and butter 338
Miso soup with tofu 51
Oat Congee 162
Oatmeal soup with spring onion and carrots 134
Polenta with ratatouille 225
Potato cream with herbs and fresh cheese 217

Potato pancakes 893
Potato-basil soup 95
Refreshing cucumber soup with potatoes 148
Ribbon noodles with leaf spinach 722
Roasted barley patties 398
Roasted millet with Celery sticks 400
Rosemary Potatoes.. 188
Semolina soup with vegetables 105
Tea Green tea.. 2
Vegetable bowl with tofu and curry on rice.................................... 162
Vegetable miso soup with tofu... 106
Vegetable rice 303

4 Snack

Adzuki Bean and Rice Soup... 199
Carrot and potato rucola sandwich 94
Cream cheese substitute.. 526
Polenta with ratatouille 225

5 Lunch

Adzuki Bean and Rice Soup... 199
Andalusian fish pot.. 347
Antipasti... 100
Asparagus Cream Soup... 240
Barley and vegetable soup 281
Barley soup.. 265
Bean paste piquant sweet 311
Beef pumpkin and vegetable stew... 369
Beef salad.. 249
Beluga lentil stew with vegetables 201
Black beans with avocado.. 263
Black root with yogurt.. 424
Boiled fillet with potatoebiscuits (Austrian classic Tafelspitz).......... 453
Broccoli cream soup.. 98
Bulgur with tomatoes and fresh herbs... 205
Carp soup 499
Carrot and potato rucola sandwich 94
Carrot Risotto... 308
Champignon rice.. 410
Champignon salad with cress.. 220
Chicken in an ilalian style 410
Chicken soup with green spelt, parsley and sake.......................... 150

Chicken with white turnips on rice... 323
Classic ginger chicken with rice wine... 357
Cod soup with tomatoes.. 176
Colorful tuscan bean soup.. 249
Corn coffee with cardamom... 3
Couscous Salad... 338
Cream cheese substitute... 526
Dal - spicy lentils... 323
Delicately spiced zucchini with tomatoes 203
Fennel and potato gratin 147
Fennel with roasted walnuts... 342
Fennel-Rice Soup 155
Fine Russian borscht 171
Fish soup with rosemary 271
Grilled lamb chops with sweetpotatorpuree and leafy vegetables... 914
Grilled salmon steaks with cauliflower and potatoes 329
Grilled tomatoes with cheese filling... 469
Hearty polenta mash... 262
Hungarian rice salad 421
Italian champignon rice 256
Kohlrabi in chervil sauce with potatoes.. 187
Lasagne with tofu cream 301
Legumes... 31
Lettuce with fresh cheese.. 802
Lettuce with vinegar dressing 67
Marinated cod on pumpkin puree 201
Millet with egg and butter 338
Miso soup with tofu 51
Oat Congee 162
Oatmeal soup with spring onion and carrots 134
Oven potatoes with celery-curd cheese (quark)............................. 304
Pancakes with spinach and parmesan.. 329
Paprika turkey with rice and lettuce 391
Polenta with ratatouille 225
Potato bags with wild herbs and tomato sauce 417
Potato cream with herbs and fresh cheese 217
Potato gnocchi with vegetables and basil sauce 166
Potato pancakes 893
Potato-basil soup 95
Potatoes with wild garlic-curd cheese.. 254
Quick zucchini soup 41
Refreshing cucumber soup with potatoes 148
Ribbon noodles with leaf spinach 722

Rice congee with chicken liver and buckthorn fruit........................ 175
Rice pesto with pine nuts 274
Roasted barley patties 398
Roasted millet with Celery sticks 400
Rosemary Potatoes.. 188
Russian kasha with white cabbage....................................... 250
Salmon on tomato-spinach.. 364
Semolina soup with vegetables 105
Sliced lamb with rosemary potatoes 461
Spinach with Tahini.. 150
Spring salad... 162
Stew with sweet potato and leeks...................................... 316
Sweet potato pancakes with basil pesto 625
Tea Green tea... 2
Tofu-Black Bean Chili with Rice.. 343
Turkey breast with vegetables (Asian).................................. 535
Vegetable bowl with tofu and curry on rice............................. 162
Vegetable miso soup with tofu.. 106
Vegetable rice... 303
Yellow lentil soup 155
Zucchini with basil pesto 467

6 Afternoon

Carrot and potato rucola sandwich 94

7 Dinner

Adzuki Bean and Rice Soup.. 199
Andalusian fish pot.. 347
Asparagus Cream Soup 240
Barley and vegetable soup.. 281
Barley soup.. 265
Beef pumpkin and vegetable stew....................................... 369
Beef salad... 249
Beluga lentil stew with vegetables 201
Black beans with avocado... 263
Black root with yogurt... 424
Boiled fillet with potato biscuits (Austrian classic Tafelspitz)........... 453
Broccoli cream soup.. 98
Carp soup 499
Carrot Risotto... 308
Champignon salad with cress... 220
Chicken in an ilalian style 410

Chicken with white turnips on rice.. 323
Classic ginger chicken with rice wine... 357
Cod soup with tomatoes... 176
Corn coffee with cardamom.. 3
Cream cheese substitute.. 526
Delicately spiced zucchini with tomatoes 203
Fennel and potato gratin 147
Fennel with roasted walnuts 342
Fennel-Rice Soup 155
Fine Russian borscht 171
Fish soup with rosemary 271
Grilled lamb chops with sweetpotatorpuree and leafy vegetables... 914
Grilled salmon steaks with cauliflower and potatoes 329
Grilled tomatoes with cheese filling... 469
Hearty polenta mash.. 262
Hungarian rice salad 421
Kohlrabi in chervil sauce with potatoes.. 187
Lasagne with tofu cream 301
Lettuce with vinegar dressing 67
Marinated cod on pumpkin puree 201
Miso soup with tofu 51
Oat Congee 162
Oven potatoes with celery-curd cheese (quark)............................. 304
Pancakes with spinach and parmesan... 329
Paprika turkey with rice and lettuce 391
Polenta with ratatouille 225
Potato gnocchi with vegetables and basil sauce 166
Potato-basil soup 95
Quick zucchini soup 41
Refreshing cucumber soup with potatoes 148
Ribbon noodles with leaf spinach 722
Rice congee with chicken liver and buckthorn fruit........................ 175
Rice pesto with pine nuts 274
Roasted barley patties 398
Roasted millet with Celery sticks 400
Rosemary Potatoes.. 188
Russian kasha with white cabbage.. 250
Salmon on tomato-spinach.. 364
Semolina soup with vegetables 105
Sliced lamb with rosemary potatoes 461
Spinach with Tahini.. 150
Stew with sweet potato and leeks.. 316
Sweet potato pancakes with basil pesto 625

Tea Green tea.. 2
Tofu-Black Bean Chili with Rice....................................... 343
Turkey breast with vegetables (Asian).......................... 535
Vegetable bowl with tofu and curry on rice.................. 162
Vegetable miso soup with tofu.. 106
Yellow lentil soup 155
Zucchini with basil pesto 467

8 Any time

Corn coffee with cardamom... 3
Lettuce with vinegar dressing 67
Miso soup with tofu 51
Oat Congee 162
Polenta with ratatouille 225
Roasted millet with Celery sticks 400
Semolina soup with vegetables 105
Tea Green tea... 2

9   Recipes

(recommendable) = You can use more.
(little) = You should use less than specified or omit.

9.1   Adzuki Bean and Rice Soup

Strengthens spleen, heart, kidney and stomach, supports urination, improves blood circulation, reduces inflammation.
Cooking time approx. 2 hours
Calories p. portion: 199
1 portions
Allergens:

Quantity of ingredients:
Adzuki beans 8 table spoons / 40g. (yes)
Rice round grain 2 table spoons / 20g. (yes)
Water 1 1/2 cups / 200g. (yes)
Honey 1 table spoon / 8g. (yes)

Cooking instructions:
Boil soaked adzuki beans and round grain rice in a ratio of 4: 1 in water until a thin pulp has formed. Sweet as needed; possibly puree.

Effect: This recipe strengthens kidney, spleen and stomach and is particularly suitable for mothers with too little milk flow.

9.2   Andalusian fish pot

Strengthens immune system, prevents cancer, dissolves stagnation, promotes weight loss. Good to fight immunodeficiency, loss of appetite, flatulence, high blood pressure, depressions, diabetes, diarrhea, stimulates appetite.
Cooking time approx. 30 min
Calories p. portion: 348
4 portions
Allergens: ADLO

Quantity of ingredients:
Basic recipe for a vegetable soup (nutritious) 2 cups / 500g. (yes)
Onion (spring onion) 2 pieces / 40g. (little)
Olive oil 1 table spoon / 20g. (yes)
Lemon peel 1/2 piece / 3g. (little)
Bay leaf 1 piece / 1g. (yes)

Potato 5/8 oz / 200g. (yes)
Cod 3/4 lbs / 300g. (recommended)
White wine 4 table spoons / 80g. (little)
Lemon juice 1/2 teaspoon / 10g. (little)
Salt 1 pinch / 1g. (little)
Pepper (ground) 1 pinch / 0,2g. (yes)
Parsley 1 table spoon / 15g. (yes)
White bread (wheat bread) 8 slices / 250g. (little)

Cooking instructions:
Boil the vegetable broth with small spring onion, olive oil, grated lemon
peel and bay leaf. Boil covered for 10 minutes. Add the peeled, diced
potatoes and boil in about 8 minutes. Add fish pieces and white wine
and switch to small heat. In the slightly boiling broth put the fish and boil
it a few minutes. Season with lemon juice, salt and pepper. Serve with
parsley sprinkled.
White bread as a side dish.

9.3   Antipasti

Improves blood circulation, anti-inflammatory, relieves pain. Diuretic,
promotes digestion, reduces blood pressure. antioxidativ, antibacterial,
affects anorexia, improves digestion, flatulence, stomach weakness,
stimulating.
Cooking time approx. 40 min
Calories p. portion: 100
3 portions
Allergens:

Quantity of ingredients:
Pepperoni 1 piece / 5g. (yes)
Lemon juice 1 table spoon / 10g. (little)
Aubergine 1 piece / 300g. (yes)
Tomato 4 pieces / 200g. (recommended)
Zucchini 5/8 oz / 200g. (recommended)
Lemon peel 1/2 piece / 3g. (little)
Olive oil 1 table spoon / 15g. (yes)
Basil (fresh) 8 leaves / 5g. (yes)
Salt 1 pinch / 0,5g. (little)
Coriander 1/2 teaspoon / 2g. (yes)

Cooking instructions:
Preheat the oven to 250 degrees Celsius and bake the hot peppers until the bowl becomes dark (about 20
minutes). Cover the hot peppers with a clear film and allow to cool. Peel the skin and cut into strips about 2 cm wide. Cut tomatoes in half and spread with oil in slices of aubergine and bake in the oven at 200 degrees golden brown (about 10 minutes)
Fry the zucchini slices in the grill pan (without fat).
Mix everything together, mix the marinade of olive oil, salt and lemon peel and pour over the vegetables, sprinkle with coriander. Leave for 1 hour.

9.4   Asparagus Cream Soup

Diuretic, improves blood circulation, prevents cancer, laxative, antiparasitic, stimulates liver function, good to fight loss of appetite, flatulence, rheumatism, heartburn.
Cooking time approx. 45 min
Calories p. portion: 240
2 portions
Allergens: ACG

Quantity of ingredients:
Asparagus (green or white) 5/8 oz / 200g. (recommended)
Water 2 cup / 500g. (yes)
Rapeseed oil 2 table spoons / 30g. (recommended)
Wheat flour 2 table spoons / 10g. (yes)
Chicken yolk 1 piece / 25g. (little)
Cow's milk (whole milk 3.5% fat) 1 table spoon / 15g. (yes)
Sour cream 15% fat 1 table spoon / 15g. (yes)
Pepper (ground) 1 pinch / 0,5g. (yes)
Nutmeg 1 pinch / 0,5g. (yes)
Lemon juice 1 teaspoon / 2g. (little)
Parsley 2 table spoons / 20g. (yes)
Salt 1 pinch / 1g. (little)

Cooking instructions:
Wash and peel the asparagus.
Heat water, a little lemon juice and pinch of salt till it boils. Tie the asparagus spears together.
Add the asparagus peel to the cooking water and bring to the boil.
Add the asparagus and cook on low heat for about 20 minutes.
Then remove the asparagus bunches and pour the broth through a

sieve.

For the roux, heat the oil in a saucepan, add the flour and sauté until it is colorless, slowly top up with the asparagus sauce and simmer for 10 minutes.

Cut the asparagus spears into pieces about 3 cm long and place them to the soup.

Just before serving, bring the soup to the boil again.
Mix the egg yolk with the milk and sour cream.
Remove the pot from the heat and stir in the egg yolk and milk mixture.
Season with pepper and nutmeg, decorate with the chopped parsley and serve immediately.

9.5   Barley and vegetable soup

Supports urination, detoxifying, promotes spleen and liver, reduces blood pressure, strengthens immune system, prevents cancer, reduces radiation damage, promotes digestion, helps to digest fat, harmonizes metabolism.

Cooking time approx. 2 hours
Calories p. portion: 281
3 portions
Allergens: AGL

Quantity of ingredients:
Barley 1 cup / 120g. (yes)
Shiitake, dried 1/8 oz / 4g. (yes)
Onion (shallot) 1 piece / 20g. (little)
Cumin (Caraway seed) 1 knife tip / 0,5g. (yes)
Sunflower oil 1 table spoon / 10g. (yes)
Water 1 cup / 250g. (yes)
Celery sticks 2 branches / 20g. (recommended)
Peas, green 5/8 lbs - 8oz / 250g. (yes)
Tomato 1 piece / 50g. (recommended)
Carrot 2 pieces / 150g. (recommended)
French beans Handful / 30g. (yes)
Salt 1 pinch / 1g. (little)
Pepper (ground) 1 pinch / 0,5g. (yes)
Parsley 1 teaspoon / 3g. (yes)
Butter organic 1 teaspoon / 3g. (yes)

Cooking instructions:
Soak the barley in the evening for the next day. Soak the mushrooms separately at the next day. Brown onion and cumin in oil, then boil with water. Add the chopped vegetables, some salt, the barley and the shiitake mushrooms and cook everything to a thick soup. At the end, season with pepper, parsley and a little butter.

9.6 Barley soup

Diuretic, forcing spleen, supports urination, stimulates liver function, antioxidativ, promotes digestion, detoxifying, reduces blood lipids, stimulates, dissolves stagnation.
Cooking time approx. 25 min
Calories p. portion: 265
2 portions
Allergens: A

Quantity of ingredients:
Barley 1 cup / 120g. (yes)
Salt 1 pinch / 1g. (little)
Ginger fresh 1/2 teaspoon / 1g. (yes)
Olive oil 1 table spoon / 10g. (yes)
Parsley 2 table spoons / 30g. (yes)
Water 1 1/2 cups / 240g. (yes)

Cooking instructions:
Roast the barley in the pan, then grind it to the ground, and boil with water, some salt and ginger to a mash. Before serving add oil and parsley.

Variant: You can add a better taste to the dish if you cook it with prepared vegetable or meat broth.

9.7 Basic recipe for a beef broth (clear)

Strengthens muscles, tendons and bones, reduces blood pressure, strengthens immune system, prevents cancer, reduces radiation damage, stimulates digestion, reduces pain, promotes digestion, diuretic. Rosemary stimulates digestion.
Cooking time approx. 4-8 hours
Calories p. portion: 114
10 portions
Allergens: O

Quantity of ingredients:
Beef soup meat 1,1 lbs / 500g. (yes)
Beef meatbones 5/8 oz / 200g. (yes)
Vinegar (Red wine vinegar) 1 dash / 3g. (yes)
Juniper berry 8 pieces / 6g. (recommended)
Rosemary 1 pinch / 1g. (yes)
Carrot 3 pieces / 210g. (recommended)
Parsnip 2 pieces / 300g. (yes)
Leek 1 piece / 200g. (yes)
Ginger fresh 1/2 teaspoon / 5g. (yes)
Lovage 1 stem / 15g. (yes)
Clove 2 pieces / 2g. (yes)
Pimento 6 pieces / 12g. (yes)
Anise (Common Fennel) 2 pieces / 1g. (yes)
Salt 1 teaspoon / 5g. (little)
Water 3,3 lbs / 1300g. (yes)

Cooking instructions:
Heat water, a dash of red wine vinegar, some juniper berries, a little rosemary, bones and meat till it boils; add carrot, parsnip, leek, ginger, lovage, clove, allspice, star anise and a little salt; simmer for 4-8 hours then strain. Refrigerate for later use.

9.8   Basic recipe for a chicken broth worming

Strengthens blood, strengthens bone marrow, reduces blood pressure, strengthens immune system, reduces radiation damage, promotes sweating, dissolves stagnation, good to fight loss of appetite, flatulence.
Cooking time approx. 2-3 hours
Calories p. portion: 90
9 portions
Allergens: L

Quantity of ingredients:
Chicken meat 1/2 piece / 600g. (yes)
Carrot 2 pieces / 150g. (recommended)
Leek 1 stick / 45g. (yes)
Celery root 1 piece / 500g. (recommended)
Ginger fresh 2 slices / 2g. (yes)
Fenugreek (Trigonella foenum-graecum) 1 teaspoon / 2g. (yes)
Juniper berry 1 teaspoon / 3g. (recommended)
Bay leaf 3 pieces / 2g. (yes)
Water 4 cup / 900g. (yes)

Cooking instructions:
Remove chicken parts from fat. Place chicken pieces in a saucepan with hot water and heat till it boils briefly, skimming any resulting foam. Add coarsely chopped vegetables and all spices and cook over medium heat for 2 to 3 hours. Strain the finished soup. Throw away vegetables and bones.
Tip: If you want to use the meat as a soup insert, take out after 45 minutes and return only the bones in the soup.
Refrigerate for later use.

9.9 Basic recipe for a duck broth

Forcing spleen, strengthens blood, supports urination, reduces blood pressure, strengthens immune system, prevents cancer, reduces radiation damage.
Cooking time approx. 2-3 hours
Calories p. portion: 61
6 portions
Allergens: L

Quantity of ingredients:
Duck (heart) 5/8 oz / 200g. (yes)
Water 2 cup / 450g. (yes)
Duck (slaughtered) 1/4 lbs - 4oz / 100g. (yes)
Carrot 2 pieces / 100g. (recommended)
Celery root 1/2 piece / 600g. (recommended)

Cooking instructions:
Cook duck pieces with vegetables for 2-3 hours. Sift broth through a fine sieve and refrigerate for later use.

The innards can be reused: You cut them finely and leaves them for a few minutes with fresh vegetables in the broth draw. Sprinkle with parsley before serving.

9.10 Basic recipe for a fish broth

Strengthens the kidneys, promotes watering, reduces blood pressure, strengthens immune system, prevents cancer, reduces radiation damage. Low in cholesterol and protein rich. Improves blood circulation, stimulates appetite.
Cooking time approx. 40 min
Calories p. portion: 128

5 portions
Allergens: DLO

Quantity of ingredients:
Fish pieces mixed (fresh water) 3/4 lbs / 300g. (recommended)
Celery root 1/4 lbs - 4oz / 120g. (recommended)
Leek 2 inches / 10g. (yes)
Carrot 2 pieces / 150g. (recommended)
White wine 1/2 cup / 125g. (little)
Lemon 1/2 piece / 50g. (little)
Bay leaf 2 leaves / 2g. (yes)
Peppercorns 3 pieces / 2g. (yes)
Olive oil 1 table spoon / 10g. (yes)
Water 2 cup / 450g. (yes)

Cooking instructions:
Fry celery, chopped carrots and leeks in olive oil, add bay leaf and peppercorns, add pieces of fish and sauté briefly. Add water, add little white wine or lemon. Simmer gently for 30 minutes. Skim off the resulting foam several times. In the end, sift the ingredients through a cloth. Refrigerate for later use

9.11 Basic recipe for a reissue soup (Congee)

Low fat content, for the drainage of the body overweight and high blood pressure.
Cooking time approx. 2-4 hours
Calories p. portion: 140
3 portions
Allergens:

Quantity of ingredients:
Rice variety any 1 cup / 120g. (yes)
Water 6 cups / 700g. (yes)

Cooking instructions:
Cook rice and water in a ratio of about 1: 6. The amount of water determines the thickness of the mash (matter of taste).
Put the rice in a saucepan with a heavy lid. It is important to simmer the rice after a short boil on the slightest flame, otherwise it burns.
Boil the rice for 2-4 hours. The longer he cooks, the more he strengthens.
If you want to eat the dish for breakfast, you can put the rice on just

before bedtime.
To be on the safe side, you should first check the behavior of your pot and cooker under observation for a similar amount of time, so that nothing burns. Refrigerate for later use.

9.12 Basic recipe for a vegetable soup, nutritious

Reduces blood pressure, strengthens immune system, prevents cancer, forcing spleen, dissolves stagnation, promotes weight loss. Good to fight immunodeficiency, high blood pressure, depressions, diabetes, diarrhea, reduces blood lipids.
Cooking time approx. 2-3 hours
Calories p. portion: 48
5 portions
Allergens: L

Quantity of ingredients:
Olive oil 1 table spoon / 4g. (yes)
Onion white 1 piece / 60g. (little)
Carrot 3 pieces / 200g. (recommended)
Parsnip 3/8 lbs - 6oz / 150g. (yes)
Celery root 1 cup / 100g. (recommended)
Ginger fresh 1/2 teaspoon / 2g. (yes)
Lemon 1/2 piece / 25g. (little)
Juniper berry 6 pieces / 6g. (recommended)
Thyme dried 1 pinch / 1g. (yes)
Lovage 1 table spoon / 3g. (yes)
Bay leaf 2 leaves / 1g. (yes)
Salt 1 pinch / 1g. (little)
Water 3 cups / 650g. (yes)

Cooking instructions:
Cut the vegetables into cubes.
Heat oil in hot pot, fry shortly onions and vegetables.
Add cold water, then add ginger, bay leaf and lemon juice.
Season with juniper, thyme and lovage. Cover for 2 - 3 hours on a low heat and simmer.
The used vegetables should be thrown away.
The basic recipe serves as a soup base and to refine vegetables, legumes or cereals.
If you want to eat vegetable soup immediately, add the desired vegetables half an hour before.
Refrigerate for later use.

9.13 Bean paste piquant sweet

Supports urination, lowers cholesterol, prevents arteriosclerosis, antioxidativ. Promotes digestion, helps to digest fat, supports urination, reduces blood pressure.
Cooking time approx. 1 hour
Calories p. portion: 311
1 portions
Allergens: MO

Quantity of ingredients:
Black beans 1 cup / 120g. (yes)
Ginger fresh 1 inch / 3g. (yes)
Boxhorn clover seeds 1/2 teaspoon / 2g. (yes)
Tomato paste 1 table spoon / 10g. (yes)
Olive oil 2 table spoons / 20g. (yes)
Pumpkin seed oil 1 dash / 3g. (yes)
Mustard 1 knife tip / 1g. (yes)
Radish horseradish 1 teaspoon (grated) / 2g. (recommended)
Pepper (ground) 1 pinch / 0,5g. (yes)
Garlic 2 cloves / 3g. (yes)
Salt 1 pinch / 1g. (little)
Sugar molasses 2 table spoons / 20g. (little)
Lemon peel 1/2 piece / 1g. (little)

Cooking instructions:
Boil beans (with spices and ginger), drain water and puree. Season with spices.

Refine with sugar beet syrup and lemon peel.

9.14 Beef pumpkin and vegetable stew

Reduces inflammation, improves digestion, reduces blood glucose, strengthens the muscles, tendons and bones, promotes digestion, helps to digest fat.
Cooking time approx. 1 hour
Calories p. portion: 369
4 portions
Allergens: AL

Quantity of ingredients:
Beef meat 3/4 lbs / 350g. (yes)
Pumpkin 3/4 lbs / 350g. (yes)
Leek 3/8 lbs - 6oz / 150g. (yes)
Potato 3/4 lbs / 350g. (yes)
Tomato 3/8 lbs - 6oz / 150g. (recommended)
Olive oil 2 table spoons / 25g. (yes)
Basic recipe for a vegetable soup (nutritious) 1/4 lbs - 4oz / 125g. (yes)
Salt 1 pinch / 1g. (little)
Pepper (ground) 1 pinch / 0,5g. (yes)
Peppers powder 1 teaspoon / 2g. (yes)
Ground caraway 1 pinch / 1g. (yes)
Sugar cane sugar 1 pinch / 1g. (little)
Parsley 1/2 bunch / 30g. (yes)
White bread (wheat bread) 4 slices / 80g. (little)

Cooking instructions:
Dice beef. Peel pumpkin and dice. Cut the leek into rings and dice the peeled potatoes.
Brew the tomatoes with boiling water, peel off the skin and dice.
Steam the meat in olive oil and fill with vegetable stock. Add the cleaned vegetables. Season with salt, pepper, paprika, cumin and fructose.
Stew for 30 minutes over low heat.
Season again and sprinkle with parsley and serve with white bread.

9.15 Beef salad

Strengths spleen and stomach, strengthens blood, strengthens the muscles, tendons and bones, diuretic, detoxifying, suppresses conversion of sugar into fat, lowers cholesterol, dissolves stagnation.
Cooking time approx. 10 min
Calories p. portion: 249
1 portions
Allergens: O

Quantity of ingredients:
Beef meat 1/8 lbs - 2oz / 50g. (yes)
Onion white 1/2 oz / 20g. (little)
Peppers 1 oz / 30g. (recommended)
Cucumber (spicy cucumber) 1 oz / 30g. (recommended)
Vinegar (Apple vinegar) 2 teaspoons / 5g. (yes)

Rapeseed oil 2 teaspoons / 5g. (recommended)
Salt 1 pinch / 0,5g. (little)
Pepper (ground) 1 pinch / 0,1g. (yes)
Chives 1 table spoon / 7g. (yes)
Bread with carob kernel flour 2 slices / 50g. (yes)

Cooking instructions:
Cook the meat with the basic recipe of a beef broth and let it cool down.
Cut into 1 cm slices. Cut the onions into rings, pepper and gherkin into
small cubes. Mix all ingredients.
Make the salad marinade with vinegar, oil and salt and pour over,
season to taste and strain.

9.16 Beluga lentil stew with vegetables

Promotes sweating, dissolves stagnation. Relieves constipation,
strengthens mother milk production, stimulates nerves, detoxifying,
reduces inflammation, improves blood circulation. Strengthens heart
and kidney, diuretic, calms the stomach, promotes digestion.
Cooking time approx. 20 min
Calories p. portion: 201
5 portions
Allergens:

Quantity of ingredients:
Lentils 1 1/2 cups / 240g. (recommended)
Water 4-5 cups / 500g. (yes)
Carrot 3 pieces / 150g. (recommended)
Leek 1 piece / 300g. (yes)
Kohlrabi 1/2 piece / 200g. (recommended)
Tomato 2 pieces / 80g. (recommended)
Onion white 1 piece / 50g. (little)
Bay leaf 2 leaves / 1g. (yes)
Fennel 1 piece / 250g. (recommended)
Star anise 2 pieces / 1g. (yes)
Juniper berry 6 pieces / 2g. (recommended)
Olive oil 2 table spoons / 30g. (yes)
Salt 1 pinch / 1g. (little)
Ginger fresh 1/2 teaspoon / 2g. (yes)
Black caraway 1 pinch / 1g. (yes)

Cooking instructions:
Heat oil in hot pot. Fry onions and add diced vegetables and spices, lentils (washed well) and salt. Cover with cold water (3 fingers wide) and cook for 20 minutes on a low heat.
Sprinkle with fresh herbs and black cumin
Goes well with rice!

9.17 Black beans with avocado

Anti-inflammatory, good to fight swelling and pain. Supports urination, lowers cholesterol, prevents arteriosclerosis, improves blood circulation, strengthens the muscles. Promotes digestion, detoxifying, promotes perspiration, reduces blood lipids, stimulates, dissolves stagnation.
Cooking time approx. 1 hour
Calories p. portion: 264
3 portions
Allergens: EN

Quantity of ingredients:
Black beans 1 cup / 100g. (yes)
Water 4 cups / 450g. (yes)
Lemon 1 dash / 1g. (little)
Boxhorn clover seeds 1 pinch (powder) / 0,2g. (yes)
Sesame oil 1 table spoon / 10g. (recommended)
Ginger fresh 1 teaspoon / 2g. (yes)
Wakame 1 inch / 1g. (yes)
Soy sauce 1 dash / 1g. (yes)
Avocado 1 piece / 300g. (yes)

Cooking instructions:
Preparation the day before:
Soak 2 cups of black beans in about 6 cups of cold water for 6-8 hours and then strain.
Put the black beans in 4 cups of fresh cold water; add a dash of lemon juice, some fenugreek seed powder, 1 tablespoon of sesame oil, 1 teaspoon of grated ginger; add a piece of wakame or 1 tbsp of hijiki. Simmer for about 45 minutes; puree with the blender; season with plenty of soy sauce.
In the morning:
Peel ½ avocado per serving and cut into small boats; Serve with the warm bean paste.
Note: The black beans can be pre-cooked for 2 - 3 days to be used as breakfast or other meals with little effort.

9.18 Black root with yogurt

Stimulates kidney, bladder and forces the cleaning of the body. In the physiological sense, they generally stimulate the glands in the organism. Good to fight acute or chronic constipation of the intestine. Rich in Vitamins and trace elements.
Cooking time approx. 20 min
Calories p. portion: 424
2 portions
Allergens: AG

Quantity of ingredients:
Salsify 1 lbs / 400g. (yes)
Yogurt (natural, 1.5% fat) 4 table spoons / 80g. (recommended)
Herbs various 1 table spoon / 8g. (yes)
Salt 1 pinch / 1g. (little)
Herbs various 2 table spoons / 6g. (yes)
Multi-grain bread (gray bread) 6 slices / 120g. (yes)

Cooking instructions:
Peel the salsify and simmer in salted water until tender. Pour away the water, cool the salsify and cut it to size.
Cover with yoghurt and sprinkle with fresh herbs. Serve with the bread. You can also use the salsify from the conserve.

9.19 Boiled fillet with potato (Austrian classic Tafelspitz)

Strengths spleen and stomach, strengthens blood, strengthens the muscles, tendons and bones. Improves digestion, regenerates skin, supports urination, lowers cholesterol.
Cooking time approx. 3 hours
Calories p. portion: 454
8 portions
Allergens: L

Quantity of ingredients:
Onion white 1 piece / 50g. (little)
Corn germ oil 1 table spoon / 10g. (recommended)
Water 32 cup - 1 gallon / 0g. (yes)
Beef meat 5,4 lbs - 70oz cap of rump / 1800g. (yes)
Beef meatbones 4n slices with bone marrow / 0g. (yes)
Salt 1 pinch / 0,5g. (little)

Peppercorns 15 pieces / 0g. (yes)
Parsnip 1 piece / 0g. (yes)
Carrot 2 pieces / 0g. (recommended)
Celery root 1 slice / 0g. (recommended)
Parsley root 2 pieces / 0g. (yes)
Leek 1/2 stick / 0g. (yes)
Chives 1 table spoon (chopped) / 7g. (yes)
Potato 2,2 lbs / 1000g. (yes)
Sunflower oil 2 table spoons / 20g. (yes)
Salt 1 pinch / 0,5g. (little)

Cooking instructions:
Halve the onions, but do not peel. Brown onions in a pan with fat on the cut surfaces very dark. Wash meat and bones briefly with warm water, drain.
Heat the water till it boils, put in meat and cook gently. Always scoop up rising foam. As soon as no more foam rises, add peppercorns and the onion. Clean and cut root and leeks and add after about two and a half hours cooking time. Simmer for another half hour.
Remove boiled beef from the soup, pour through a sieve and season with salt. Cut roots into bite-sized pieces.
Add the soup together with the marrow bones and leave it under the boiling point. Cut the boiled beef into finger-thick slices against the grain, place in the soup, heat again, sprinkle with a little chives.
In addition, cook and peel the potatoes in salted water. Stomp roughly or cut finely. Fry in a pan with the oil crispy.

9.20 Broccoli cream soup

Strengthen your immune system, build and maintain healthy bones, teeth, hair and nails. Reduces blood pressure, strengthens immune system, prevents cancer, reduces radiation damage.
Cooking time approx. 30 min
Calories p. portion: 98
6 portions
Allergens: LO

Quantity of ingredients:
Olive oil 2 table spoons / 7g. (yes)
Broccoli 1,1 lbs / 500g. (recommended)
Carrot 2 pieces / 150g. (recommended)

Potato 2 pieces / 120g. (yes)
Onion white 1 piece / 50g. (little)
Water 1 cup / 50g. (yes)
Basic recipe for a vegetable soup (nutritious) 2 cup / 500g. (yes)
White wine 1/2 cup / 125g. (little)
Sage 1 teaspoon / 2g. (yes)
Rosemary 1 teaspoon / 2g. (yes)
Pepper (ground) 1 pinch / 0,5g. (yes)
Salt 1 pinch / 1g. (little)

Cooking instructions:
Add the olive oil to the pan, add the washed and cut broccoli, diced carrots and potatoes, sauté for a short time, add the chopped onion, fill with water, enough water to cover the vegetables at least 3 finger breadths. Add bouillon, salt, add a little bit of white wine, add the seasoned sage and rosemary.
Heat till it boils and then simmer on a small fire for about 25 minutes.
Season with pepper, if necessary season with sea salt. Purée the soup.

9.21 Bulgur with tomatoes and fresh herbs

Promotes digestion, helps to digest fat, supports urination, reduces blood pressure. Stimulates digestion, supports urination.
Cooking time approx. 30 min
Calories p. portion: 205
1 portions
Allergens: A

Quantity of ingredients:
Bulgur (cereals) 1 cup / 120g. (yes)
Tomato 2 pieces / 70g. (recommended)
Rucola 2 table spoons / 16g. (recommended)
Pepper powder (hot) 1 pinch / 2g. (yes)
Olive oil 2 table spoons / 20g. (yes)
Pepper (ground) 1 pinch / 0,5g. (yes)
Salt 1 pinch / 1g. (little)
Basil 4 leaves / 2g. (yes)
Thyme 1 Twig / 3g. (yes)
Lemon juice 1/2 piece / 10g. (little)

Cooking instructions:
Put cold water in a pot, sprinkle in Bulgur and simmer. Stir in chopped tomatoes, fresh herbs like basil, thyme, arugula, a pinch of rose paprika, lemon juice, a dash of olive oil, a little ground pepper, some salt.

Variant: add some mozzarella.

Recommendation: ideal morning meal in summer; also suitable as evening meal, especially for sleep disorders.

9.22 Carp soup

Increase milk production and sweating, dissolves stagnation, reduces blood pressure, strengthens immune system, improves blood circulation, improves medication effect, stimulates appetite. Strengthens gastrointestinal function, expands blood vessels.
Cooking time approx. 2 hours
Calories p. portion: 499
2 portions
Allergens: DO

Quantity of ingredients:
Carp 1,1 lbs / 500g. (yes)
Salt 1 pinch / 1g. (little)
Vinegar (Apple vinegar) 1 teaspoon / 3g. (yes)
Thyme 1 Twig / 3g. (yes)
Juniper berry 8 pieces / 3g. (recommended)
Carrot 2 pieces / 200g. (recommended)
Leek 1 piece / 200g. (yes)
Onion white 1 piece / 60g. (little)
Ginger fresh 1/2 teaspoon / 2g. (yes)
Bay leaf 3 leaves / 1g. (yes)
White wine 1/2 cup / 125g. (little)
Basil 3 leaves / 1g. (yes)

Cooking instructions:
Preparation: When shopping at the fishmonger, remove the fillets from a medium-sized, whole carp and also pack the fish head, spine with bones and tail.
Cut the fillets into 1 cm cubes; salt and set aside.

Place fish head, backbone and tail of carp in plenty of cold water; heat till it boils and scoop the foam; add a dash of vinegar, a fresh sprig of thyme, juniper berries; Add carrot, a piece of leek and chopped onion; add a thick slice of ginger, some peppercorns, 1 bay leaf, salt; simmer for about 1 1/2 hours and pour the stock through a sieve.

Put the carp pieces in a saucepan; pour a shot of white wine; Add rose paprika, basil leaves, finely ground carrots, dried thyme and the stock and warm; Boil the ingredients for about 5 minutes until the fish pieces are cooked.
Variants: Thicken the soup with kudzu or mashed potatoes.
This fits: baguette and dry white wine.

9.23 Carrot and potato rucola sandwich

Reduces inflammation, improves digestion, supports urination, lowers cholesterol, strengthens immune system, prevents cancer, good to fight constipation (Fibre-rich), dissolves stagnation.
Cooking time approx. 20 min
Calories p. portion: 94
4 portions
Allergens: AG

Quantity of ingredients:
Potato (mealy) 5/8 oz / 200g. (yes)
Carrot 1 piece / 50g. (recommended)
Sour cream 15% fat 2 table spoons / 45g. (yes)
Onion (spring onion) 1 piece / 20g. (little)
Rucola 1/2 bunch / 100g. (recommended)
Lemon peel 1/4 teaspoon / 1g. (little)
Salt 1 pinch / 1g. (little)
Pepper (ground) 1 pinch / 0,2g. (yes)
Whole grain bread 8 slices / 48g. (recommended)

Cooking instructions:
Cook the potatoes gently, peel and squeeze through the potato press.
Cook vegetable broth according to the basic recipe and remove a carrot after a short cooking time and finely crush with a fork.
Stir the potatoes, carrots, grated lemon zest and sour cream into a smooth cream.
Mix carrot and potato cream with finely chopped rocket salad. Season the spread with salt and pepper and spread the bread. Sprinkle with the finely chopped young onions.

9.24 Carrot Risotto

Strengthens immune system, prevents cancer, loss of appetite, flatulence, high blood pressure, depressions, diabetes, diarrhea, stimulates liver function, dissolves stagnation.
Cooking time approx. 45 min
Calories p. portion: 308
2 portions
Allergens: GL

Quantity of ingredients:
Olive oil 1/2 teaspoon / 5g. (yes)
Onion (spring onion) 2 table spoons / 7g. (little)
Nutmeg 1 pinch / 0,3g. (yes)
Parsley 1/2 bunch / 25g. (yes)
Rice variety any 1/4 lbs - 4oz / 100g. (yes)
Carrot 5/8 lbs - 8oz / 250g. (recommended)
Basic recipe for a vegetable soup (nutritious) 1 cup / 280g. (yes)
Fennel seeds ground 1/4 teaspoon / 1g. (yes)
Basil (fresh) 1/2 teaspoon / 2g. (yes)
Salt 1 pinch / 1g. (little)
Pepper (ground) 1 pinch / 0,3g. (yes)
Parmesan 1 table spoon / 10g. (yes)

Cooking instructions:
Heat the oil in a pan, fry the onions in a glassy and very soft manner. Add parsley, sauté briefly. Add rice, carrots and nutmeg, sauté briefly while stirring. Add the vegetable stock, season with fennel and basil, heat till it boils and cook for about 20 minutes until the rice and carrots are well. Stir from time to time and add some vegetable stock if necessary. The risotto should be slightly soupy. Just before the end of the cooking time mix in the white wine and simmer the risotto for a short while. Remove risotto from the heat, mix in Parmesan.

9.25 Champignon rice

Strengthens kidney, diuretic, warming the body from the inside, expands blood vessels, strengthens the muscles, promotes digestion and is good to fight high blood pressure, dissolves stagnation, promotes weight loss. Good to fight immunodeficiency, loss of appetite.
Cooking time approx. 30 min
Calories p. portion: 410
2 portions
Allergens: L

Quantity of ingredients:
Onion white 1 piece / 50g. (little)
Bay leaf 2 pieces / 1g. (yes)
Clove 2 pieces / 1g. (yes)
Basic recipe for a vegetable soup (nutritious) 7/8 lbs / 350g. (yes)
Rice (whole grain) 5/8 oz / 200g. (recommended)
Champignon 1/8 lbs - 2oz / 60g. (yes)
Parsley 1/2 oz / 20g. (yes)
Pepper (ground) 1 pinch / 0,2g. (yes)

Cooking instructions:
Plug in the cloves in the onion. Heat the vegetable stock with the onion and the bay leaves till it boils. Add the rice to the boiling liquid, reduce the temperature to the lowest level and stir with the lid closed for 20-25 minutes.
In the meantime, wash the mushrooms, clean them, slice them, sauté briefly with a little water or sauté. Wash the parsley and chop finely.
Remove the onion from the rice, add the mushrooms and the parsley, season with pepper.

9.26 Champignon salad with cress

Promotes digestion and is good to fight high blood pressure. Good to fight loss of appetite, improves blood circulation.
Cooking time approx. 5 min
Calories p. portion: 220
1 portions
Allergens: AN

Quantity of ingredients:
Champignon 5/8 lbs - 8oz / 250g. (yes)
Sesame oil 2 table spoons / 6g. (recommended)
Pepper (ground) 1 pinch / 0,5g. (yes)
Salt 1 pinch / 1g. (little)
Lemon 1/2 piece / 15g. (little)
Peppers powder 2 pinches / 0,1g. (yes)
Cress 2 table spoons / 10g. (yes)
White bread (wheat bread) 2 slices / 30g. (little)

Cooking instructions:
Cut mushrooms into thin slices.
Dressing: sesame oil, a little ground pepper, salt, plenty of lemon juice, stir well the rose pepper; give over the finely chopped mushrooms; plenty of watercress.
Goes well with: white bread, round grain rice or quinoa; Along with the cereal, the salad makes a simple, light meal.
Serve with white bread.

9.27 Chicken in an ilalian style

Strengthens bone marrow, improves blood circulation, strengthens the muscles, antioxidativ. Basmati rice: To drain the body overweight and high blood pressure.
Cooking time approx. 1 hour
Calories p. portion: 410
4 portions
Allergens: M

Quantity of ingredients:
Olive oil 2 table spoons / 30g. (yes)
Chicken meat 1 piece (cut into 8 pieces) / 700g. (yes)
Garlic 3 cloves / 5g. (yes)
Rosemary 1/2 teaspoon / 2g. (yes)
Salt 1 pinch / 1g. (little)
Pepper (ground) 1 pinch / 0,5g. (yes)
Water 1 cup / 20g. (yes)
Rice Basmati 1 cup / 120g. (yes)
Water 6 cups / 400g. (yes)
Salt 1 pinch / 1g. (little)
Lettuce 1 piece / 300g. (recommended)
Olive oil 2 table spoons / 20g. (yes)
Lemon juice 1/4 piece / 7g. (little)
Mustard 1 pinch / 3g. (yes)
Salt 1 pinch / 1g. (little)
Honey 1 pinch / 2g. (yes)

Cooking instructions:
In a heavy pan (with lid) heat 1 tbsp of olive oil at low temperature. Add the chicken pieces and fry for a few minutes. Once they start to take on color, add the remaining 2 tablespoons of olive oil and garlic. Turn the chicken parts in the oil and sprinkle with rosemary, salt and pepper. Pour with a little water and heat till it boils. Reduce the heat, put on the

lid and stew the chicken for 35 to 45 minutes.

In between, check again and again whether there is enough cooking water, and if necessary, add 1 to 2 tablespoons of water each time.

As soon as the meat comes off the bone, spread the chicken parts on the plates, deglaze the roast residue in the braised pan with a few tablespoons of water or wine and spread over the meat as a sauce.

In the meantime, cook the rice in a saucepan with (1:6) salted water, on a low heat.

Wash and spin the lettuce, finely chop and serve in a bowl. In a small bowl, mix the olive oil, lemon juice, mustard, salt and honey well and add to the salad and add it to the salad.

9.28 Chicken soup with green spelt, parsley and sake

Strengthens blood, strengthens bone marrow, reduces blood pressure, strengthens immune system, stimulates liver function, detoxifying. Improves blood circulation, improves medication effect, stimulates appetite.
Cooking time approx. 1 1/2 hours
Calories p. portion: 150
2 portions
Allergens: AL

Quantity of ingredients:
Basic recipe for a chicken soup (warming) 2 cup / 500g. (yes)
Green spelt 4 table spoons / 30g. (yes)
Parsley 2 table spoons / 14g. (yes)
Sake 1 dash / 2g. (yes)

Cooking instructions:
Cook the chicken broth according to the basic recipe. Add the ingredients in the soup and simmer 10 min.

9.29 Chicken with white turnips on rice

Strengthens bone marrow. Rice to drain the body at overweight and high blood pressure.
Cooking time approx. 45 min
Calories p. portion: 324
4 portions
Allergens: GL

Quantity of ingredients:
Butter organic 2 table spoons / 20g. (yes)
Olive oil 2 table spoons / 20g. (yes)
Onion white 1 piece / 60g. (little)
Turnips 4 pieces / 200g. (recommended)
Garlic 2 pieces / 3g. (yes)
Basic recipe for a chicken soup (warming) 1 cup / 100g. (yes)
Parsley 2 table spoons / 15g. (yes)
Salt 1 pinch / 1g. (little)
Olive oil 1 teaspoon / 4g. (yes)
Chicken meat 7/8 lbs / 400g. (yes)
Water 6 cups / 400g. (yes)
Rice Basmati 1 cup / 120g. (yes)

Cooking instructions:
In a heavy pot, heat the butter and the oil at low temperature. Add the onion, stir and simmer for about 20 minutes on very low heat until soft and golden brown. Add the chopped beets and the chopped garlic cloves and stir well.
Add the chicken broth or water, add some salt and heat till it boils. Reduce the heat, put on the lid and simmer the beets for about 20 minutes. Look in between if there is still enough liquid in the pot, and if necessary, pour in a few tablespoons of chicken stock. At the end there should be very little liquid in the pot. Remove the lid and allow the remaining liquid to evaporate, stirring constantly.

In the meantime roast the finely chopped chicken pieces in a frying pan with a little oil. Finally, sprinkle with a little chili and fry for another minute while constantly turning.
Serve the pieces of chicken, turnips and rice on the plates, spread the sauce over them and sprinkle with parsley immediately.
Cook the rice in the ratio of 6 cups of water: 1 cup of rice.

Small, fresh, untreated beets do not need to be peeled. Otherwise, peel beets and place in hot water for 10 minutes. This makes them easier to digest and lose some of their sharp, pungent odor. White turnips are rich in vitamin C, potassium and folic acid.

9.30 Classic ginger chicken with rice wine

Forcing spleen, blood and bone marrow. Relieves fatigue, regulates gastrointestinal function. Diuretic, building up, eye-enhancing, detoxifying, nerve-strengthening.
Cooking time approx. 30 min
Calories p. portion: 357
4 portions
Allergens: GO

Quantity of ingredients:
Butter organic 2 table spoons / 30g. (yes)
Ginger fresh 2 table spoons / 18g. (yes)
Salt 1 pinch / 0,5g. (little)
Chicken meat 2 pieces (legs) / 500g. (yes)
Lychee liqueur 1 dash / 2g. (little)
Curry 1 pinch / 1g. (yes)
Sake 1 dash / 1g. (yes)
Corn 4 table spoons / 30g. (yes)
Millet 1/2 cup / 50g. (yes)
Salt 1 pinch / g. (little)
Water 1 1/2 cups / 200g. (yes)
Lettuce 1/2 piece / 100g. (recommended)
Olive oil 1 table spoon / 10g. (yes)
Vinegar (Apple vinegar) 1 teaspoon / 3g. (yes)
Water 2 table spoons / 20g. (yes)
Salt 1 pinch / 0,5g. (little)
Herbs various 1 table spoon / 8g. (yes)

Cooking instructions:
Heat butter in a hot pan (preferably made of cast iron or enamel); sauté chopped ginger (about 1 heaped tablespoons per chicken leg) on low heat; add some salt, chicken and/or other parts of the chicken and roast all around with gentle heat; add Lychee liqueur or maple syrup, add a little curry and fry for a short time; stir in plenty of sake; add corn kernels (from the glass, health food trade); boil all the ingredients in the sauce for a few minutes, until the meat is cooked; season with salt. This fits: millet, lettuce or lettuce.

9.31 Cod soup with tomatoes

Promotes spleen and kidney; promotes watering. Strengthens the kidneys. Improves blood circulation, improves medication effect, stimulates appetite, helps to digest fat, supports urination, reduces blood pressure, stimulates liver function, detoxifying.
Cooking time approx. 30 min
Calories p. portion: 176
4 portions
Allergens: DLO

Quantity of ingredients:
Basic recipe for a fish soup 2 cup / 450g. (yes)
Cod 5/8 lbs - 8oz / 250g. (recommended)
Onion (shallot) 1 piece / 20g. (little)
Anise (Common Fennel) 1/2 teaspoon / 1g. (yes)
Ginger fresh 1/2 teaspoon / 1g. (yes)
Olive oil 1 teaspoon / 3g. (yes)
Tomato 1 piece / 50g. (recommended)
White wine 1/2 cup / 125g. (little)
Salt 1 pinch / 0,5g. (little)
Pepper (ground) 1 pinch / 0,2g. (yes)
Parsley 1 table spoon (chopped) / 5g. (yes)

Cooking instructions:
Fry the onion, anise and freshly grated ginger in oil.
Add finely chopped tomatoes and sauté. Add a little wine and fish soup. Simmer gently for 10-15 minutes. Season with salt and pepper; Add the cod pieces and heat gently. Garnish with parsley at the end.

9.32 Colorful tuscan bean soup

Promotes digestion, helps to digest fat, supports urination, reduces blood pressure, diuretic, calms the stomach.
Cooking time approx. 2 hours
Calories p. portion: 249
3 portions
Allergens: L

Quantity of ingredients:
Kidney beans (red) 1/8 lbs - 2oz / 50g. (yes)
Chickpeas 1 oz / 25g. (yes)
Lentils 1 oz / 25g. (recommended)
Celery sticks 1 stick / 10g. (recommended)

Tomato 2 pieces / 100g. (recommended)
Fennel seeds ground 1/2 teaspoon / 1g. (yes)
Salt 1 pinch / 1g. (little)
Pepper (ground) 1 pinch / 0,5g. (yes)
Garlic 1 clove / 3g. (yes)
Olive oil 2 table spoons / 50g. (yes)
Water 2 1/4 cups / 500g. (yes)
Basil (fresh) 5-7 leaves / 3g. (yes)

Cooking instructions:
Soak legumes, boil and puree. Add vegetables, spices, herbs and oil and cook gently for 2 hours.

Variation: Sweet chestnuts give the dish a special Italian touch.

9.33 Corn coffee with cardamom

Diuretic, forcing spleen, supports urination, relaxes, reduces fat.
Cooking time approx. 5 min
Calories p. portion: 3
1 portions
Allergens:

Quantity of ingredients:
Cereal coffee 1 table spoon / 15g. (yes)
Cardamom 2 cores / 1g. (yes)
Water 1 cup / 120g. (yes)

Cooking instructions:
Boil water, coffee, sugar and cardamom. Let it set for one min before drinking.

9.34 Couscous Salad

prevents cancer, forcing spleen, promotes digestion, stimulates liver function, reduces blood pressure, strengthens immune system, reduces radiation damage, diuretic.
Cooking time approx. 25 min
Calories p. portion: 338
3 portions
Allergens: A

Quantity of ingredients:
Water 1 cup / 100g. (yes)
Olive oil 1 table spoon / 15g. (yes)
Couscous 5/8 oz / 200g. (yes)
Lemon juice 2 table spoons / 30g. (little)
Lemon peel 1 teaspoon / 2g. (little)
Tomato 2 pieces / 80g. (recommended)
Cucumber 1/4 lbs - 4oz / 100g. (recommended)
Carrot 1/4 lbs - 4oz / 100g. (recommended)
Parsley 1 Bunch / 100g. (yes)
Chives 1 Bunch / 100g. (yes)
Peppermint 3 twigs / 30g. (yes)

Cooking instructions:
Boil in a small saucepan 250 ml. water with salt and 1 tablespoon olive oil. Add the couscous, take the stove in the front and let it swell covered for 5 minutes. Put the couscous back on the stove and let it simmer for about 2 minutes with gentle stirring. If necessary, add 1 - 3 tbsp of hot water.
Mix the couscous with lemon juice, chopped lemon peel and 1 tbsp oil, season with salt and pepper and leave to set.
Add couscous with tomatoes, cucumber, parsley (all diced), carrots (grated), chives and mint (finely chopped).
Season the couscous salad with lemon juice, salt and pepper.

9.35 Cream cheese substitute

Good to fight lactose intolerance. Strengthens body energy, promotes digestion, promotes weight loss. Good to fight immunodeficiency, loss of appetite, arteriosclerosis, flatulence, bladder weakness, anemia, high blood pressure, depressions, diabetes, diarrhea.
Cooking time approx. 20 min
Calories p. portion: 526
2 portions
Allergens: AE

Quantity of ingredients:
Soybean milk 4 cup / 300g. (yes)
Lemon 1 piece / 50g. (little)
Herbs various 2 table spoons / 6g. (yes)
Whole grain bread 6 slices / 300g. (recommended)

Cooking instructions:
Heat the soy milk in a saucepan till it boils, stirring occasionally (gets burn easily!), Then allow to cool.
Squeeze out the lemon and stir gently under the cooled soy milk (approx. 80°C/176°F), let it approx. 20 min. rest or clot.
Pour chopped soy milk through a strainer lined with a dishcloth, allow liquid to drain and then squeeze out remaining liquid with the dishcloth.
Refine to taste with fresh herbs.
Serve with wholemeal bread.

9.36 Dal - spicy lentils

Strengthens heart and kidney, diuretic, calms the stomach, promotes digestion. Strengthens gastrointestinal function, expands blood vessels, prevents cancer, prevents diseases (in the elderly).
Cooking time approx. 45 min
Calories p. portion: 323
2 portions
Allergens:

Quantity of ingredients:
Lentils yellow 5/8 lbs - 8oz / 400g. (yes)
Onion white 2 pieces / 120g. (little)
Ginger fresh 1 thumb large / 4g. (yes)
Garlic 2-3 cloves / 6g. (yes)
Clarified butter 3-4 table spoons / 30g. (little)
Curry 3-4 teaspoons / 8g. (yes)
Pork fat (lard) 1 table spoon / 10g. (yes)
Garam Masala powder 1 teaspoon / 3g. (yes)
Salt 1 pinch / 1g. (little)

Cooking instructions:
Wash the lentils carefully and soak for at least 1/2 hour before starting to boil (unpeeled whole lentils should soak for 1 or better for 2 hours, in halves the time may be significantly shorter). Peel onions and finely dice, as well as the garlic cloves. Peel the ginger, either chop very finely or, better and easier, grate on a fine grater.
Give Ghee in a very hot saucepan, then add the onion cubes and simmer for 2 minutes while stirring. Then reduce the temperature a little and continue to fry until the onions are golden brown. Then add the garlic and after another minute the ginger. Reduce the temperature to half and continue roasting for 1-2 minutes while stirring. Then add the curry powder and let it simmer for about 1-2 minutes in hot fat. Also add

the Garam Masala and let it melt for a short time. If the spices stick on the bottom of the pot, you can solve them again with very little water. Remove half of the onion spice mixture from the pot and set aside. Increase the heat again and add the soaked lentils (without the soaking water) and simmer for 2-3 minutes with stirring. Then add water until the lenses are covered with liquid (approx. 750 ml). When the water boils, reduce the heat and simmer the lentils slowly until soft. Stir occasionally and add water if necessary. Cooking takes 30-70 minutes, depending on the type of lentil and soaking time.

When the lentils are soft, stir in the rest of the onion mixture and season with not too much salt. Let it rest for at least 10 minutes. Then serve with rice or flatbread.

9.37 Delicately spiced zucchini with tomatoes

Diuretic, promotes digestion, helps to digest fat, dissolves stagnation, antioxidativ, warming the body from the inside, expands blood vessels.
Cooking time approx. 10 min
Calories p. portion: 203
4 portions
Allergens:

Quantity of ingredients:
Olive oil 1 table spoon / 20g. (yes)
Onion white 2 pieces / 120g. (little)
Zucchini 4 pieces / 800g. (recommended)
Oregano dried 1 pinch / 1g. (yes)
Basil (fresh) 6-8 leaves / 3g. (yes)
Salt 1 pinch / 1g. (little)
Tomato 2 pieces / 120g. (recommended)
Rice (whole grain) 1 cup / 120g. (recommended)
Water 6 cups / 400g. (yes)
Salt 1 pinch / 1g. (little)

Cooking instructions:
In a hot pan, fry olive oil, finely chopped onions and finely chopped zucchini until half cooked. Add plenty of dried oregano. Salt and chop the tomatoes for a few minutes until the zucchini are tender but crisp. Add fresh basil as desired.
Variation: Put some sheep's cheese over the tomatoes and finish cooking with the lid closed.
Place the rice in salted water, heat till it boils and let it simmer over low heat for about 15 minutes.

9.38 Fennel and potato gratin

Reduces inflammation, improves blood circulation, improves digestion, supports urination, lowers cholesterol, good to fight loss of appetite, flatulence, inflammatory bowel disease, heartburn. Forcing spleen, improves blood circulation.
Cooking time approx. 1 1/2 hours
Calories p. portion: 147
2 portions
Allergens: CGL

Quantity of ingredients:
Fennel 5/8 oz / 200g. (recommended)
Potato 1/4 lbs - 4oz / 125g. (yes)
Basic recipe for a vegetable soup (nutritious) 1/2 cup / 100g. (yes)
Butter organic 1 teaspoon / 3g. (yes)
Rice flour 2 teaspoons / 6g. (yes)
Cream sour 10% 1 teaspoon / 3g. (yes)
Salt 1 pinch / 1g. (little)
Sugar cane sugar 1 pinch / 1g. (little)
Chicken yolk 1 piece / 10g. (little)
Pepper Cayenne 1 pinch / 0,5g. (yes)
Nutmeg 1 pinch / 0,5g. (yes)
Parsley 1 teaspoon / 2g. (yes)
Chives 1 teaspoon / 3g. (yes)
Parmesan 1 teaspoon / 3g. (yes)
Butter organic 1 teaspoon / 3g. (yes)

Cooking instructions:
Cook peeled potatoes and then let cool. Wash the fennel, cut off the stems and remove any outer leaves.
Hold back fennel greens and add it to the sauce with the other herbs later.
Steam the fennel tubers for about 15 - 20 minutes.
Then cut the potatoes and fennel into slices and place in layers in a greased baking dish.
Bring the liquid of fennel broth to the boil and bind it with flour.
Season with sea salt, cayenne pepper, sugar, nutmeg and sour cream. Allow to cool and alloy with egg yolk.
Spread the sauce over the casserole, sprinkle with parmesan and finely chopped parsley and chives. Bake at 200 °C / 392 °F in the oven for half an hour.

9.39 Fennel with roasted walnuts

Forcing spleen, detoxifying, reduces inflammation, improves blood circulation, improves medication effect, stimulates appetite, antioxidativ, promotes digestion, stimulates, dissolves stagnation.
Cooking time approx. 20 min
Calories p. portion: 342
4 portions
Allergens: HO

Quantity of ingredients:
Fennel 4 pieces / 800g. (recommended)
Nutmeg 1 pinch / 1g. (yes)
Ginger fresh 1/2 teaspoon / 1g. (yes)
Salt 1 pinch / 1g. (little)
White wine 1/2 cup / 125g. (little)
Peppers powder 1 pinch / 1g. (yes)
Olive oil 2 table spoons / 40g. (yes)
Walnuts 2 table spoons / 35g. (recommended)
Water 1 1/2 cups / 220g. (yes)
Corn Grease (Polenta) 1 cup / 120g. (yes)
Salt 1 pinch / 1g. (little)

Cooking instructions:
Heat very little water in a pot; Fry the fennel in strips. Add Nutmeg, a little grated ginger, add salt, a dash of white wine, rose paprika.
Simmer until the vegetables are cooked, but still crisp; stir in a little olive oil; sprinkle with roasted walnuts.

Stir the polenta into a pot of hot water, stirring constantly, until the polenta has the desired consistency. Salt.
Pull the polenta off the fire and let it swell for about 10 minutes.

9.40 Fennel-Rice Soup

Forcing spleen, relieves constipation, stimulates nerves, detoxifying, reduces inflammation, improves blood circulation.
Cooking time approx. 15-20 min
Calories p. portion: 156
2 portions
Allergens: EG

Quantity of ingredients:
Basic recipe for a rice soup (Congee) 1 cup / 300g. (yes)
Fennel 1/2 piece / 150g. (recommended)
Butter organic 1 table spoon / 15g. (yes)
Soy sauce 1 dash / 3g. (yes)

Cooking instructions:
Cook the fennel softly in the rice soup according to the basic recipe.
Before serving, add a piece of butter and some soy sauce.

9.41 Fine Russian borscht

Strengths spleen and stomach, strengthens the heart, stimulates
digestion, reduces blood pressure, strengthens immune system. For
strengthening after diseases. Good to fight bloating, cramping in
gastrointestinal complaints.
Cooking time approx. 30 min
Calories p. portion: 172
6 portions
Allergens: AGLO

Quantity of ingredients:
Red beet 5/8 oz / 200g. (recommended)
Sunflower oil 1 table spoon / 10g. (yes)
Onion (shallot) 2 pieces / 40g. (little)
Carrot 2 pieces / 140g. (recommended)
Celery root 1 piece / 500g. (recommended)
Parsley root 1 piece / 150g. (yes)
Leek 1/8 lbs - 2oz / 50g. (yes)
Basic recipe for a vegetable soup (nutritious) 3 cups / 650g. (yes)
Bay leaf 1 Leaf / 0,2g. (yes)
Juniper berry 2 pieces / 2g. (recommended)
Nutmeg 1 pinch / 1g. (yes)
Savoy cabbage / kale 5/8 oz / 200g. (recommended)
Salt 1 pinch / 1g. (little)
Pepper (ground) 1 pinch / 0,5g. (yes)
Ground 1 pinch / 1g. (yes)
Red wine 1/2 cup / 125g. (little)
Sour cream 15% fat 1 table spoon / 10g. (yes)
Dill 1 teaspoon / 10g. (yes)
White bread (wheat bread) 6 slices / 120g. (little)

Cooking instructions:
Fry some beetroot in oil. Fry the onions, carrots, celery, parsley root and leek well in another pan. Add the stock and the wine; then add bay leaves, juniper berries and nutmeg and simmer for 15 minutes. Remove the bay leaf and puree everything.
Heat more broth separately, simmer the steamed beetroot in it. Add cabbage or white cabbage after half the cooking time and let it steep. At the end, add the pureed vegetables and season with salt, pepper, ground cumin
and a little red wine. Garnish with some sour cream and finely chopped dill in the plate. Serve with a slice of white bread.

9.42 Fish soup with rosemary

Promotes spleen and liver, reduces blood pressure, strengthens immune system, prevents cancer, reduces radiation damage, has little cholesterol and is protein rich, improves blood circulation, increases appetite. Antioxidant, forcing spleen, dissolves stagnation.
Cooking time approx. 30 min
Calories p. portion: 271
4 portions
Allergens: DLO

Quantity of ingredients:
Basic recipe for a fish soup 2 cup / 500g. (yes)
Rosemary 1/2 bunch / 7g. (yes)
Onion (spring onion) 1 piece / 20g. (little)
Olive oil 2 table spoons / 35g. (yes)
Fish pieces mixed (fresh water) 5/8 lbs - 8oz / 250g. (recommended)
Carrot 1 piece / 120g. (recommended)
Parsnip 1 piece / 180g. (yes)
Celery root 1 slice / 20g. (recommended)
Salt 1 pinch / 1g. (little)
Peppercorns 2 pieces / 1g. (yes)
Garlic 1 clove / 3g. (yes)

Cooking instructions:
Fry the onion and garlic in oil. Add fish broth. Add diced carrots, parsnips and celery. Season with salt and peppercorns. Simmer the soup on a low heat for 25 minutes.
Wash the fish, drizzle with lemon juice, divide into pieces and add to the soup with the pink rosemary. Cook for 5 min on low heat.
Add the chives and parsley and season the soup with the salt.

9.43 Grilled lamb chops with sweet potato puree & vegetables

Relieves weakness, strengthens lung, spleen and stomach.
Strengthens the immune system, reduces fat, improves digestion.
Cooking time approx. 45 min
Calories p. portion: 914
2 portions
Allergens: E

Quantity of ingredients:
Lamb meat 6 pieces (chops) / 300g. (yes)
Garlic 2 cloves / 3g. (yes)
Rosemary 2 table spoons / 5g. (yes)
Salt 1 pinch / 1g. (little)
Olive oil 2 table spoons / 20g. (yes)
Sweet potato 3/4 lbs / 300g. (yes)
Basil 1 table spoon / 3g. (yes)
Soybean milk 1/4 lbs - 4oz / 100g. (yes)
Basil 1 table spoon / 3g. (yes)
Salt 1 pinch / 1g. (little)
Nutmeg 1 pinch / 0,5g. (yes)
Pepper (ground) 1 pinch / 0,5g. (yes)
Chard 2 handful / 20g. (yes)
Spinach 2 handful / 20g. (yes)
Savoy cabbage / kale 2 handful / 20g. (recommended)
White cabbage 2 handful / 20g. (recommended)
Herbs various Handful / 10g. (yes)
Olive oil 2 table spoons / 20g. (yes)
Salt 1 pinch / 1g. (little)
Pepper (ground) 1 pinch / 0,5g. (yes)

Cooking instructions:
Lamb chops:
Preheat the oven grill to about 180°C/365°F and set the shelf to a height, such that the chops are about 8 to 12 centimeters from the heat source. Remove the most fat of the chops and place them in a fireproof mold. Rub the meat first with garlic, then with the rosemary salt mixture and spread a few teaspoons of olive oil over it.
Turn the lamb chops once so that they are covered with oil on both sides, put them under the grill and grill on both sides for 5 to 7 minutes or until the meat is well browned.

Mashed sweet potatoes:
Peel all sweet potatoes and cut into large cubes, boil gently in salted water and strain. Leave to soak in the 100°C/212°F hot brook for a few minutes. Remove the basil leaves. Puree sweet potatoes.
Approximately Boil 1/8 l soymilk with basil once, then strain a little and strain and mix with the passed sweet potatoes. Season with salt, pepper and nutmeg. Depending on the consistency of the puree, add a little more milk.

Steamed leafy vegetables:
After the season chard, spinach, savoy cabbage, white cabbage, fresh herbs and the mugwort in a pot with olive oil softly. Season with salt and pepper

9.44 Grilled salmon steaks with cauliflower and potatoes

Improves digestion, regenerates skin, supports urination, lowers cholesterol, supports digestion.
Cooking time approx. 30 min
Calories p. portion: 330
4 portions
Allergens: D

Quantity of ingredients:
Garlic 1 clove / 1g. (yes)
Onion (shallot) 1/2 piece / 5g. (little)
Lemon juice 1 dach / 1g. (little)
Salt 1 pinch / 1g. (little)
Cauliflower 1 piece / 500g. (recommended)
Olive oil 2 table spoons / 20g. (yes)
Garlic 1 clove / 1g. (yes)
Water 2/3 cup / g. (yes)
Parsley 2 table spoons / 15g. (yes)
Potato 1,1 lbs / 500g. (yes)
Salt 1 pinch / 1g. (little)
Salmon 4 pieces (steaks) / 500g. (recommended)
Lemon 1/2 piece / 2g. (little)

Cooking instructions:
Garlic shallots mixture:
Finely squeeze the garlic, finely chop the shallots, add a dash of lemon

juice and salt and stir. Mix with a little oil to a paste.

Cauliflower:
Cut the cauliflower into pieces.
Heat the oil in a heavy saucepan and fry the crushed garlic for a short time.
Add the cauliflower pieces and turn in the oil. Add a little water and cook until the cauliflower is firm. Strain the cauliflower and cook the remaining water until a thick sauce remains. Add the cauliflower and crush it roughly with a wooden spoon. Add the chopped parsley and salt.

Potatoes:
Cook the potato in a saucepan with plenty of water, strain and peel.

Salmon Steak:
Preheat the oven at about 180°C/356°F. Rub in the salmon slices with the garlic-scarlet mixture and grill as close as possible to the heat source for 4 to 8 minutes from both sides. You are done when the meat is easy to divide when you pierce with a fork.
Serve and sprinkle with lemon slices and the chopped parsley.

9.45 Grilled tomatoes with cheese filling

Promotes digestion, helps to digest fat, supports urination, reduces blood pressure, stimulates digestion.
Cooking time approx. 30 min
Calories p. portion: 470
2 portions
Allergens: ACG

Quantity of ingredients:
Tomato 8 pieces / 200g. (recommended)
Feta cheese 0,2 lbs / 75g. (yes)
Fresh cheese 0,2 lbs / 75g. (yes)
Chicken egg 1 piece / 60g. (yes)
Olive oil 1 table spoon / 12g. (yes)
Basil (fresh) 1 table spoon / 6g. (yes)
Salt 1 pinch / 1g. (little)
Pepper (ground) 1 pinch / 0,5g. (yes)
Olives 1 oz / 30g. (yes)
Rucola 1/4 lbs / 100g. (recommended)
White bread (wheat bread) 4 slices / 80g. (little)

Cooking instructions:
Hollow out tomatoes generously. Put in a casserole dish.
Mix cheese, olive oil, egg, chopped basil and flour. Season with salt and pepper and fill in the tomatoes.
Bake in the preheated oven at 210 degrees on the middle rail for 15 minutes, then switch on the oven grill and grill for a further 3 minutes (without circulating air).
Stone the olives and chop and sprinkle on the tomatoes.
Garnish tomatoes with rocket and serve with white bread.

9.46 Hearty polenta mash

Strengths spleen and stomach, promotes watering, promotes digestion, detoxifying, promotes perspiration, reduces blood lipids, stimulates, dissolves stagnation, stimulates appetite, dissolves stagnation.
Cooking time approx. 10 min
Calories p. portion: 262
2 portions
Allergens:

Quantity of ingredients:
Corn Grease (Polenta) 1 cup / 120g. (yes)
Onion (spring onion) 2 pieces / 40g. (little)
Ginger fresh 1/2 teaspoon / 2g. (yes)
Nutmeg 1 pinch / 1g. (yes)
Salt 1 pinch / 1g. (little)
Olive oil 1 table spoon / 10g. (yes)
Turmeric (yellow root) 1 pinch / 1g. (yes)
Water 1 1/2 cups / 240g. (yes)

Cooking instructions:
Stir in the polenta in boiling water and let it swell for 7 min. Add green onion, grated ginger, turmeric, nutmeg, salt and olive oil and wait for 3 more minutes.

9.47 Hearty winter breakfast

Strengthens immune system, calms nerves and stomach, promotes digestion, detoxifying, strengthens bodily production, promotes perspiration, reduces blood lipids, stimulates, dissolves stagnation.
Cooking time approx. 20 min
Calories p. portion: 678
1 portions
Allergens: ACEG

Quantity of ingredients:
Oat meal 1 cup / 120g. (yes)
Ginger fresh 1/2 teaspoon / 1g. (yes)
Salt 1 pinch / 1g. (little)
Onion (spring onion) 2 pieces / 40g. (little)
Chicken egg 1 piece / 55g. (yes)
Butter organic 1 table spoon / 15g. (yes)
Soy sauce 1 dash / 3g. (yes)

Cooking instructions:
Soak oatmeal overnight. Boil in the morning with a little ginger, salt and
a spring onion or leek and then let it swell until the porridge is soft.
Before serving, add a whole egg to the porridge, add the butter and
season to taste with a little soy sauce.

Recommendation: Especially suitable for the cold season.

9.48 Hungarian rice salad

Promotes digestion, helps to digest fat, supports urination, reduces
blood pressure, strengthens kidney and bladder, diuretic, warming the
body from the inside, expands blood vessels, strengthens the muscles,
regulates internal organs functions.
Cooking time approx. 25 min
Calories p. portion: 421
2 portions
Allergens: GM

Quantity of ingredients:
Rice (whole grain) 1/2 cup / 60g. (recommended)
Water 3 cups / 300g. (yes)
Salt 1 pinch / 0,3g. (little)
Tomato 1/4 lbs - 4oz / 100g. (recommended)
Peppers 1/8 lbs - 2oz / 50g. (recommended)
Champignon 1 oz / 30g. (yes)
Edam cheese 1 oz / 30g. (yes)
Yogurt (natural, 1.5% fat) 1/8 lbs - 2oz / 45g. (recommended)
Salt 1 pinch / 1g. (little)
Herbs various 1 table spoon / 8g. (yes)
Rapeseed oil 2 table spoons / 20g. (recommended)
Mustard 1 teaspoon / 3g. (yes)
Pepper (ground) 1 pinch / 0,2g. (yes)

Cooking instructions:
Pour the rice into plenty of boiling salt water and let it drain gently.
Wash tomatoes and peppers and core. Cut both in to small cubes. Peel
the mushrooms (from the tin or with rapeseed oil for a short time) and
cut the cheese into small cubes and add to the rice. Prepare the
marinade and mix with the ingredients, refrigerate and leave for at least
an hour.

9.49 Italian champignon rice

Refreshing and nourishing. Promotes digestion and is good to fight
high blood pressure. Strengthens spleen and stomach, strengthens the
muscles, improves blood circulation, encourages growth, dissolves
stagnation.
Cooking time approx. 25 min
Calories p. portion: 256
4 portions
Allergens: G

Quantity of ingredients:
Rice round grain 1 1/2 cups / 240g. (yes)
Water 2 cup / 450g. (yes)
Pepper (ground) 1 pinch / 0,2g. (yes)
Salt 1 pinch / 0,5g. (little)
Lemon juice 1 dash / 2g. (little)
Champignon 5/8 lbs - 8oz / 250g. (yes)
Pepper powder (hot) 1 pinch / 0,2g. (yes)
Olive oil 1 teaspoon / 3g. (yes)
Chives 1 teaspoon / 5g. (yes)
Parmesan 2 table spoons / 20g. (yes)

Cooking instructions:
Put the round grain rice in cold water 1:6 and cook.
Add ground pepper, salt, plenty of lemon juice, rose paprika, a little
olive oil or butter and mix well.
Carefully add in mushrooms, chives or the green parts of the spring
onion, and carefully add in some grated Parmesan cheese.
Goes well with vegetables and tofu dishes, tomato sauce dishes.

9.50 Kohlrabi in chervil sauce with potatoes

Reduces inflammation, lowers cholesterol, diuretic, conducts bowel winds, strengthens immune system, prevents cancer, promotes weight loss. Good to fight loss of appetite, flatulence, high blood pressure, depressions, diabetes, diarrhea.
Cooking time approx. 1 hour
Calories p. portion: 188
4 portions
Allergens: GL

Quantity of ingredients:
Potato 6 pieces / 450g. (yes)
Basic recipe for a vegetable soup (nutritious) 1 cup / 300g. (yes)
Potato 1/4 lbs - 4oz / 100g. (yes)
Nutmeg 1 pinch / 0,2g. (yes)
Lemon peel 1/2 teaspoon / 2g. (little)
Ginger fresh 1/2 teaspoon / 2g. (yes)
Lovage 1/2 teaspoon / 2g. (yes)
Kohlrabi 3/4 lbs / 300g. (recommended)
Salt 1 pinch / 1g. (little)
Pepper (ground) 1 pinch / 0,2g. (yes)
Sour cream 15% fat 2 table spoons / 30g. (yes)
Chervil dried 1 Bunch / 80g. (yes)

Cooking instructions:
Boil the potatoes in salted water.
Bring half of the vegetable stock to boil. Add the diced potatoes, nutmeg, lemon zest, ginger and lovage. Cover the potatoes and cook for about 10 minutes until soft and puree them with a blender until they are smooth.
Bring remaining vegetable stock to boil. Cut kohlrabi into cubes and add, cover and cook for about 8 minutes. Stir in the potato sauce and heat everything briefly.
Puree with the mixing stick chervil and sour cream. Mix the chervil cream with the kohlrabi vegetables.
Serve with the cooked, peeled potatoes.

9.51 Lasagne with tofu cream

Harmonizes spleen and stomach, reduces Flatulence, protects the digestive system. Good to fight lack of appetite, flatulence, inflammatory bowel disease, stomach ulcers, rheumatism, heartburn, twelffinger intestinal ulcers.
Cooking time approx. 45 min
Calories p. portion: 301
4 portions
Allergens: ACEG

Quantity of ingredients:
Soy Tofu 7/8 lbs / 400g. (yes)
Chicken egg 2 pieces / 100g. (yes)
Onion white 2 pieces / 120g. (little)
Tomato 1/4 lbs - 4oz / 100g. (recommended)
Oregano dried 1 pinch / 1g. (yes)
Marjoram 1 pinch / 1g. (yes)
Peppers powder 1 pinch / 1g. (yes)
Salt 1 pinch / 1g. (little)
Noodles (wheat, lasagne) with egg 3/8 lbs - 6oz / 150g. (yes)
Edam cheese 1/8 lbs - 2oz / 50g. (yes)

Cooking instructions:
Tofu cream: Mix tofu with eggs, onions, small tomatoes, oregano, marjoram, peppers and some sea salt put into a smooth mass using a kitchen machine with a knife or a blender.

Lasagne: Place 1/5 of the tofu cream in a casserole dish (25x15cm), cover with 3 lasagna leaves, repeat this process twice, and then finish the last fifth of the tofu cream over the pastry plates. Sprinkle with a little grated
Edam and bake in the oven at 175°C/347°F for about 1/2 hour.

9.52 Legumes

Reduces blood pressure, strengthens immune system, prevents cancer, reduces radiation damage. Supports urination, detoxifying. Strengthens heart and kidney, calms the stomach, promotes digestion, antibacterial, calming and appetizing.
Cooking time approx. 30 min
Calories p. portion: 31
5 portions
Allergens:

Quantity of ingredients:
Pinto beans speckled 1/4 lbs - 4oz / 100g. (yes)
Lentils 1/8 lbs - 2oz / 50g. (recommended)
Peas, green 1/8 lbs - 2oz / 50g. (yes)
Water 4 cup / 1000g. (yes)
Lemon 1 slice / 2g. (little)
Juniper berry 6 pieces / 2g. (recommended)
Thyme 1 Twig / 3g. (yes)
Rosemary 1 Twig / 3g. (yes)
Carrot 1 piece / 100g. (recommended)
Savory 1-2 teaspoons / 5g. (recommended)
Ginger fresh a great piece / 3g. (yes)
Bay leaf 2-3 leaves / 1g. (yes)
Wakame 1-2 strips / 1g. (yes)

Cooking instructions:
Legumes such as beans, lentils, peas or chickpeas are soaked in plenty
of cold water for several hours to three days. The water should be
changed every 8 hours. Then pour off soaking water and wash legumes
thoroughly.

Preparation:
Cook the legumes with fresh cold water and a slice of ginger and bring
to froth. Cook without lid for about 5 minutes, scooping off the foam.
Only then add the following ingredients: a slice of lemon or lemon juice,
crush juniper berries, thyme; (possibly 1 knife tip of asafetida in case of
severe indigestion). Add savory, sage, juniper, fenugreek seeds,
carrots, bay leaves, fresh ginger, wakame algae.

Simmer on the slightest flame until beans or lentils have the desired
consistency.
This base can be stored for 3-4 days in the refrigerator.

9.53 Lettuce with fresh cheese

The bitter substances have diuretic effect and promote the blood
circulation in the digestive area. Mustard improves thyroid function,
relieves rheumatism symptoms.
Cooking time approx. 5 min
Calories p. portion: 802
1 portions
Allergens: AFM

Quantity of ingredients:
Leaf salads (bitter) 2 portions / 60g. (recommended)
Fresh cheese from soya 3/8 lbs - 6oz / 150g. (yes)
Mustard 1 knife tip / 1g. (yes)
Lemon juice 1 dash / 3g. (little)
Salt 1 pinch / 1g. (little)
Pepper (ground) 1 pinch / 0,5g. (yes)
Herbs various 2 teaspoons / 4g. (yes)
Black caraway 1 pinch / 1g. (yes)
Whole grain bread 2 slices / 40g. (recommended)

Cooking instructions:
Wash lettuce and finely pluck.
Mix 150 ml cream cheese, splashes of mustard, splashes of lemon juice, 1 clove of garlic, chopped fresh herbs, pinch of pepper and crushed black cumin and pour over. Serve with wholemeal bread.

9.54 Lettuce with vinegar dressing

Relieves fatigue, regulates gastrointestinal function, dissolves stagnation, laxative, antiparasitic, improves blood circulation, detoxifying, reduces inflammation, relieves pain.
Cooking time approx. 10 min
Calories p. portion: 68
2 portions
Allergens: O

Quantity of ingredients:
Lettuce 1 piece / 200g. (recommended)
Vinegar (Apple vinegar) 1 table spoon / 10g. (yes)
Water 1 table spoon / 10g. (yes)
Rapeseed oil 1 table spoon / 10g. (recommended)
Onion (spring onion) 1 piece / 20g. (little)
Salt 1 pinch / 0,5g. (little)
Pepper (ground) 1 pinch / 0,1g. (yes)
Chives 1 table spoon / 5g. (yes)

Cooking instructions:
Clean lettuce, wash and drain. Add the ingredients to the marinade in an extra container. Salad with marinade just before consumption. Just before, sprinkle with chives.

9.55 Marinated cod on pumpkin puree

Reduces inflammation, improves digestion, promotes spleen, lung, stomach and kidneys, diuretic, reduces blood glucose, good to fight constipation and flatulence, dissolves stagnation.
Cooking time approx. 2 hours
Calories p. portion: 202
4 portions
Allergens: DG

Quantity of ingredients:
Potato 6 pieces / 400g. (yes)
Pumpkin 5/8 oz / 200g. (yes)
Onion white 1 piece / 50g. (little)
Oregano dried 1/2 teaspoon / 1g. (yes)
Lemon juice 1/2 piece / 15g. (little)
Salt 1 pinch / 1g. (little)
Pepper (ground) 1 pinch / 0,3g. (yes)
Créme fraiche cheese 2 table spoons / 30g. (yes)
Yogurt (natural, 1.5% fat) 3/8 lbs - 6oz / 150g. (recommended)
Oregano dried 1/4 teaspoon / 1g. (yes)
Basil (fresh) 1/2 teaspoon / 2g. (yes)
Cod 3/4 lbs / 300g. (recommended)
Salt 1 pinch / 1g. (little)
Pepper (ground) 1 pinch / 0,3g. (yes)
Olive oil 1 teaspoon / 3g. (yes)

Cooking instructions:
Mix yoghurt with oregano, basil and thyme.
Wash the fish fillets, pat dry, place in a flat shape and pour over the marinade. Leave 2 hours in refrigerator.

Cook the potatoes in salted water until soft and peel.

Sauté the onion in oil until glassy, add the diced pumpkin and cook for about 10 min. Add oregano, lemon juice, salt, pepper and crème fraiche and puree with the blender.

Remove fish fillets from the marinade, drain, pat dry and salt. Coat a coated grill pan with 2 teaspoons of oil. Roast the fish fillets on both sides for 3 - 4 minutes and arrange with the potatoes on the pumpkin puree.

9.56 Millet with egg and butter

Calms nerves and stomach, soothes embryo during pregnancy.
Diuretic, building up, eye-enhancing, detoxifying, nerve-strengthening.
Stimulates liver function, detoxifying.
Cooking time approx. 25 min
Calories p. portion: 338
2 portions
Allergens: CG

Quantity of ingredients:
Millet 1 cup / 100g. (yes)
Ginger fresh 1/2 teaspoon / 1g. (yes)
Salt 1 pinch / 0,5g. (little)
Parsley 2 table spoons / 16g. (yes)
Pepper powder (hot) 1 pinch / 1g. (yes)
Chicken egg 2 pieces / 100g. (yes)
Butter organic 2 table spoons / 20g. (yes)
Nutmeg 1 pinch / 0,2g. (yes)
Water 1 1/2 cups / 200g. (yes)

Cooking instructions:
Simmer the millet with the ginger and nutmeg in the water for 5 min.
and let it swell for another 30 min.
Cook and peel 1 soft egg per person; pile up the millet on plates and
place 1 egg each in a hollow in the millet mountain; Put butter flakes
over it. Sprinkle with chopped parsley and the rose paprika.

9.57 Miso soup with tofu

Vitamins, minerals and secondary plant active ingredients, invigorating,
detoxifying, strengthens immune system, promotes digestion, forcing
spleen, containing enzymes, reduces flatulence, alginic acid detoxifies
the bowel, dissolves stagnation.
Cooking time approx. 5 min
Calories p. portion: 51
3 portions
Allergens: E

Quantity of ingredients:
Wakame 1 piece / 5g. (yes)
Miso 3-4 table spoons / 30g. (yes)
Soy Tofu 1/8 lbs - 2oz / 50g. (yes)
Water 2 cup / 500g. (yes)

Soy sauce 1 dash / 3g. (yes)
Onion (spring onion) 1/2 teaspoon / 6g. (little)

Cooking instructions:
Boil soybean seedlings, wakame algae and diced tofu for 5 minutes.
Put the miso paste in the soup plate and slowly pour over the soup.
Season with Tamari sauce. Sprinkle with cutted spring onion.

9.58 Oat Congee

Strengthens immune system.
Cooking time approx. 2-4 hours
Calories p. portion: 162
3 portions
Allergens: A

Quantity of ingredients:
Oat 1 cup / 125g. (yes)
Water 6 cups / 700g. (yes)

Cooking instructions:
Cook oats and water in a ratio of about 1: 6. The amount of water
determines the thickness of the mash (pure matter of taste). The oats
swell, so do not take much. Put the oats in a saucepan with good
insulation and a heavy lid. It is important to simmer the oats after a
short boil on the slightest flame, otherwise it burns. Cook the oat for 2-4
hours. The longer it cooks, the more he strengthens.

9.59 Oatmeal soup with spring onion and carrots

Reduces blood pressure, strengthens immune system, prevents cancer,
reduces radiation damage, stimulates digestion, reduces pain,
stimulates appetite, dissolves stagnation.
Cooking time approx. 30 min
Calories p. portion: 135
3 portions
Allergens: AG

Quantity of ingredients:
Oat 6 table spoons / 48g. (yes)
Carrot 2 pieces / 200g. (recommended)
Butter organic 1 table spoon / 15g. (yes)
Nutmeg 1 pinch / 1g. (yes)
Lovage 1 stem / 15g. (yes)

Onion (spring onion) 2 pieces / 40g. (little)
Water 2 cup / 480g. (yes)

Cooking instructions:
Roast the oats in butter, add salt and spices, pour in water and heat till it boils. After 10 min. add the grated carrots and lovage, cook for 10 minutes. Finely add chopped onion.

9.60 Oven potatoes with celery-curd cheese (quark)

Promotes spleen, reduces Inflammation, improves digestion, regenerates skin, supports urination, lowers cholesterol.
Cooking time approx. 30 min
Calories p. portion: 304
2 portions
Allergens: GL

Quantity of ingredients:
Celery root 3 oz / 80g. (recommended)
Basic recipe for a vegetable soup (nutritious) 1/2 cup / 100g. (yes)
Ground caraway 1 pinch / 0,2g. (yes)
Lemon peel 1/2 teaspoon / 1g. (little)
Salt 1 pinch / 1g. (little)
Pepper (ground) 1 pinch / 0,2g. (yes)
Lemon juice 1 teaspoon / 3g. (little)
Curd cheese 20% 5/8 oz / 200g. (recommended)
Créme fraiche cheese 1/2 teaspoon / 5g. (yes)
Potato 6 pieces / 400g. (yes)
Olive oil 2 teaspoons / 5g. (yes)
Salt 1 pinch / 1g. (little)

Cooking instructions:
Celery-curd cheese:
Mix celery with vegetable broth according to basic recipe, caraway and lemon peel. Cook for about 8 minutes until the celery is soft and the vegetable broth almost evaporated. Mix the celery vegetable broth with the lemon juice, finely, and stir until smooth. Season with salt and pepper.
Baked potatoes:
Preheat oven to 200 °C / 400 °F.
Brush the potatoes well, halve them, and place them on a baking tray with the cut surface facing up. Lightly salt the surfaces and sprinkle with oil. Fry the potatoes in the oven for about 25 minutes.

Serve the celery plug to the potatoes.

9.61 Pancakes with spinach and parmesan

Promotes bowel movement, improves blood circulation, forcing spleen and bowel, strengthens immune system, good to fight loss of appetite, flatulence, high blood pressure, depressions, diabetes, constipation, inflammatory bowel disease
Cooking time approx. 25 min
Calories p. portion: 330
6 portions
Allergens: ACGL

Quantity of ingredients:
Wholemeal flour 1/4 lbs - 4oz / 100g. (recommended)
Wheat flour 1/4 lbs - 4oz / 100g. (yes)
Chicken egg 4 pieces / 200g. (yes)
Cow's milk (whole milk 3.5% fat) 1 1/2 cups / 400g. (yes)
Salt 1 pinch / 1g. (little)
Sunflower oil 1 table spoon / 15g. (yes)
Olive oil 1 table spoon / 15g. (yes)
Onion white 1 piece / 50g. (little)
Parsley 1/2 bunch / 80g. (yes)
Basic recipe for a vegetable soup (nutritious) 1/2 cup / 150g. (yes)
Basil (fresh) 1/4 teaspoon / 1g. (yes)
Nutmeg 1 pinch / 0,3g. (yes)
Créme fraiche cheese 2 table spoons / 45g. (yes)
Spinach 1,3 lbs / 600g. (yes)
Salt 1 pinch / 1g. (little)
Pepper (ground) 1 pinch / 0,1g. (yes)
Parmesan 1/8 lbs - 2oz / 60g. (yes)

Cooking instructions:
Stir flour, eggs and milk and a pinch of salt with the whisk until smooth.
From the dough, fry pancakes crispy brown on both sides.
Heat oil in a small saucepan. Fry the finely chopped onion until tender.
Stir in chopped parsley, sauté briefly. Add the vegetable broth
according to the basic recipe, season with basil and nutmeg. Cover and
simmer for 15 minutes, add crème fraiche and finely puree.
Cook the washed, drizzled spinach with a little salt in a closed pan over
a moderate heat in 3 minutes, drain in a sieve and cut into small pieces.
Add the spinach to the sauce, heat briefly. Add parmesan in the mix.
Fill the pancakes with the cream spinach.

9.62 Paprika turkey with rice and lettuce

Strengthens blood and bone marrow.
Cooking time approx. 1 hour
Calories p. portion: 391
6 portions
Allergens: AG

Quantity of ingredients:
Olive oil 2 table spoons / 20g. (yes)
Onion white 1 piece / 60g. (little)
Peppers (rose peppers) 2 table spoons / 14g. (yes)
Chicken meat 1 piece / 800g. (yes)
Water 1 cup / 250g. (yes)
Salt 1 pinch / 1g. (little)
Spelled wholemeal flour 1 table spoon / 7g. (yes)
Sour cream 15% fat 5/8 lbs - 8oz / 250g. (yes)
Water 6 cups / 400g. (yes)
Rice Basmati 1 cup / 120g. (yes)
Salt 1 pinch / 1g. (little)
Lettuce 1 piece / 200g. (recommended)
Olive oil 2 table spoons / 20g. (yes)
Lemon juice 1/2 piece / 15g. (little)
Herbs various 2 table spoons / 6g. (yes)

Cooking instructions:
Heat the oil in a saucepan and fry the onions in a golden yellow.
Sprinkle plenty of peppers over the onion and stir well so that it does
not burn. Put the pot aside.
In a casserole, fry the chicken parts from one side; turn the meat over,
spread the onion above and fry the chicken parts from the other side.
As soon as they have taken on a deep red color, pour the vegetable
broth and heat till it boils.
Season with salt, reduce the heat and stew the chicken for 45 minutes
or until cooked.
Put the poultry parts together with cooking liquid in a bowl and set
aside.
Add 2 to 3 tbsp of flour to the casserole and gradually add the cooking
solution again, stirring constantly until the sauce is thickened.
Stir in the sour cream or yoghurt, put the poultry pieces back into the
pot and heat again well, but do not boil.
Place the rice with the salted water, bring to the boil and simmer until
the rice is tender.

Wash and dry the lettuce. Pluck small and put in a bowl.
In a cup, mix the olive oil, the lemon juice, the salt and fresh chopped herbs and pour over the salad.

9.63 Polenta with ratatouille

Forcing spleen and stomach, lets urine and bile juice flow. Diuretic, supports urination. Promotes digestion, helps to digest fat, supports urination, reduces blood pressure.
Cooking time approx. 30 min
Calories p. portion: 226
4 portions
Allergens: G

Quantity of ingredients:
Corn Grease (Polenta) 1 cup / 120g. (yes)
Water 1 1/2 cups / 240g. (yes)
Aubergine 1 piece (large) / 200g. (yes)
Zucchini 2 pieces / 500g. (recommended)
Onion white 2 pieces / 120g. (little)
Tomato 2 pieces (blended) / 200g. (recommended)
Olive oil 2 table spoons / 20g. (yes)
Salt 1 pinch / 0,5g. (little)
Parsley 1 table spoon (chopped) / 8g. (yes)
Thyme 1/2 teaspoon / 1g. (yes)
Onion (spring onion) 2 table spoons (chopped) / 12g. (little)
Basil 4 leaves / 2g. (yes)
Parmesan 2 table spoons / 20g. (yes)

Cooking instructions:
Use double the amount of water to polenta, add salt and oil and heat till it boils. Stir in polenta, stirring constantly.
Take off the fire and let it swell for 20 minutes. Meanwhile, cut the onion, fry in a saucepan with hot oil. Add the diced zucchini, tomatoes and melanzani and simmer for about 20 minutes. Add basil, thyme, salt. Coat baking tray with oil, apply polenta evenly and wait until it gets stronger.
Add the cooked ratatouille to polenta, portion and then put in the oven for a few minutes (possibly with grated parmesan).
Sprinkle with fresh parsley and finely chopped spring onion.
The valuable tip: The Polenta sections are ideal for on the go.

9.64 Potato bags with wild herbs and tomato sauce

Promotes spleen, reduces inflammation, improves digestion, good to fight loss of appetite, flatulence, inflammatory bowel disease, stimulates liver function, promotes urination, dissolves stagnation, detoxifies, supporting prostate disorders.
Cooking time approx. 45 min
Calories p. portion: 418
5 portions
Allergens: ACG

Quantity of ingredients:
Olive oil 1 table spoon / 10g. (yes)
Onion white 1 piece / 50g. (little)
Garlic 1 piece / 2g. (yes)
Tomato puree 7/8 lbs / 400g. (yes)
Salt 1 pinch / 1g. (little)
Pepper (ground) 1 pinch / 0,5g. (yes)
Cream, sweet 30% 1 table spoon / 10g. (little)
Potato 1,4 lbs / 650g. (yes)
Wheat flour 5/8 oz / 200g. (yes)
Chicken egg 1 piece / 60g. (yes)
Salt 1 pinch / 1g. (little)
Pepper (ground) 1 pinch / 0,5g. (yes)
Nutmeg 1 pinch / 0,2g. (yes)
Nettles 1/8 lbs - 2oz / 50g. (yes)
Dandelion (young plants) 1 oz / 30g. (yes)
Yarrow 1 oz / 30g. (yes)
Chervil dried 1/2 oz / 10g. (yes)
Ribworttea 1/2 oz / 10g. (yes)
Parsley 1/8 lbs - 2oz / 50g. (yes)
Olive oil 1 table spoon / 10g. (yes)
Garlic 1 piece / 2g. (yes)
Curd cheese 20% 4 table spoons / 40g. (recommended)
Mayonnaise 50% 1 table spoon / 10g. (little)
Salt (herbal) 1/2 teaspoon / 2g. (yes)
Black caraway 1 pinch / 1g. (yes)
Pepper (ground) 1 pinch / 0,5g. (yes)
Emmental cheese 1/4 lbs / 100g. (yes)

Cooking instructions:
Tomato sauce:
Heat oil. Roast diced onion briefly with crushed garlic. Add the tomato puree and let it thicken for 2 minutes while stirring, season with salt and pepper and add the cream and place in a fireproof mold.

Potato Batter:
Cook the boiled potato, drain, peel and squeeze. Mix in a bowl with flour, Parmesan, egg and spices. Roll out the dough on a lightly floured work surface and cut into 5 cm squares.

Herb Stuffing:
Chop the herbs and mix with oil, garlic, curd cheese, mayonnaise, herb salt, crushed black cumin and pepper to a creamy mass.

Put on the pastry with a spoon in the middle. Fold into a triangle, press on the edge and let the pockets soak in plenty of salted water until they float up. Add to the tomatoes, sprinkle with the grated cheese and bake in the oven until golden brown.

9.65 Potato cream with herbs and fresh cheese

Good to fight loss of appetite, constipation, bloating and nausea.
Improves digestion, supports urination, prevents cancer, forcing spleen, dissolves stagnation, relaxing and reassuring.
Cooking time approx. 25 min
Calories p. portion: 217
2 portions
Allergens: G

Quantity of ingredients:
Potato (mealy) 5/8 lbs - 8oz / 250g. (yes)
Fresh cheese 3 oz / 80g. (yes)
Yogurt (natural, 1.5% fat) 2 table spoons / 45g. (recommended)
Chives 1/2 bunch / 50g. (yes)
Basil (fresh) 1 teaspoon / 4g. (yes)
Parsley 1 teaspoon / 4g. (yes)
Dill 1/2 teaspoon / 2g. (yes)
Salt 1 pinch / 1g. (little)
Black caraway 1 pinch / 0,5g. (yes)
Pepper (ground) 1 pinch / 0,5g. (yes)

Cooking instructions:
Softly steam the potatoes in the pan, peel them and press through the potato press.
Mix cream cheese, yoghurt and herbs under the potatoes, season with salt, crushed black cumin and pepper.

9.66 Potato gnocchi with vegetables and basil sauce

Strengthens immune system, promotes weight loss. Good to fight immunodeficiency, loss of appetite, flatulence, high blood pressure. Relaxing and reassuring.
Cooking time approx. 1 hour
Calories p. portion: 167
4 portions
Allergens: ACGL

Quantity of ingredients:
Potato 5/8 lbs - 8oz / 250g. (yes)
Wheat flour 1 oz / 25g. (yes)
Wheat semolina 1/2 oz / 15g. (yes)
Chicken yolk 1 piece / 20g. (little)
Nutmeg 1 pinch / 0,2g. (yes)
Basic recipe for a vegetable soup (nutritious) 1 cup / 250g. (yes)
Celery root 1/8 lbs - 2oz / 50g. (recommended)
Lemon peel 1/2 teaspoon / 2g. (little)
Ginger fresh 1/2 teaspoon / 2g. (yes)
Nutmeg 1 pinch / 0,2g. (yes)
Basil (fresh) 1 Bunch / 125g. (yes)
Créme fraiche cheese 1 table spoon / 20g. (yes)
Salt 1 pinch / 1g. (little)
Pepper (ground) 1 pinch / 0,2g. (yes)
Carrot 1/4 lbs - 4oz / 100g. (recommended)
Zucchini 1/4 lbs - 4oz / 100g. (recommended)
Cauliflower 1/4 lbs - 4oz / 100g. (recommended)
Broccoli 1/4 lbs - 4oz / 100g. (recommended)
Salt 1 pinch / 1g. (little)

Cooking instructions:
Steam the potatoes gently, peel and pass hot through the potato press.
Process the hot potatoes with flour, semolina, egg, nutmeg and salt to a smooth dough. Let dough rest for 3o minutes.
Make small rolls (2 cm) out of the dough with flour-dusted hands, cut off 1 cm thin slices. To create the typical gnocchi shape, gently dab the

dough pieces with your thumb. Leave the gnocchi in lightly boiling salted water for 6 - 8 minutes. Lift the gnocchi out of the pot with the skimmer.

Heat the vegetable stock till it boils. Add diced celery, grated lemon peel, finely chopped ginger and 1 pinch of nutmeg. Cover and simmer for about 10 minutes. Using the blender, puree the vegetable broth, celery, chopped basil and créme fraiche into a smooth sauce. Season with salt and nutmeg.

Cut carrots, zucchini, cauliflower and broccoli into small pieces and cook covered in a sieve over steam for 8 minutes until firm.
Heat the sauce again and add to the vegetables and arrange over the gnocchi.

9.67 Potato pancakes

Promotes spleen, reduces inflammation, improves digestion, regenerates skin, supports urination, calms nerves and stomach, laxative, antiparasitic.
Cooking time approx. 15 min
Calories p. portion: 893
1 portions
Allergens: ACG

Quantity of ingredients:
Potato (mealy) 5/8 lbs - 8oz / 250g. (yes)
Wheat flour 1/2 oz / 10g. (yes)
Chicken egg 1 piece / 35g. (yes)
Rapeseed oil 2 table spoons / 20g. (recommended)
Salt 1 pinch / 1g. (little)
Cream sour 20% 1/8 lbs - 2oz / 50g. (yes)
Salt 1 pinch / 1g. (little)
Herbs various 1 table spoon / 10g. (yes)

Cooking instructions:
Grater the peeled potatoes finely, add the remaining ingredients, mix well and salt. Heat the oil and add small flat cakes to the pan with the spoon. Roast the potato pancakes on both sides crispy golden brown. Place them on the plate with sour cream, salt and sprinkle with herbs.

9.68 Potato-basil soup

Reduces inflammation, improves digestion, supports urination, lowers cholesterol, reduces blood pressure, strengthens immune system, prevents cancer, reduces radiation damage, antioxidativ, dissolves stagnation.
Cooking time approx. 25 min
Calories p. portion: 96
4 portions
Allergens: L

Quantity of ingredients:
Water 2 cups / 450g. (yes)
Potato 4 pieces / 200g. (yes)
Carrot 2 pieces / 100g. (recommended)
Celery root 1 piece / 500g. (recommended)
Pepper (ground) 1 pinch / 0,5g. (yes)
Ground 1 pinch / 1g. (yes)
Garlic 1 clove / 3g. (yes)
Salt 1 pinch / 1g. (little)
Lemon 1 teaspoon / 3g. (little)
Basil (fresh) 1 Bunch / 50g. (yes)
Peppers powder 1 pinch / 1g. (yes)
Sugar cane sugar 1 pinch / 1g. (little)
Olive oil 1 table spoon / 10g. (yes)

Cooking instructions:
Peeled and chopped 4 medium potatoes in a pot of hot water and 2 chopped medium carrots, a piece of celery root, a pinch of pepper, a pinch of ground cumin, crushed a small clove of garlic, a pinch of salt, 1 teaspoon of lemon juice, simmer until the Vegetables is soft.
Add 1 bunch finely chopped basil into one half of the soup and puree everything; stir in the other half of the basil; with rose paprika, a pinch of whole cane sugar, 1 tablespoon of olive oil or butter, freshly ground pepper, salt to taste.

9.69 Potatoes with wild garlic-curd cheese

Improves digestion, regenerates skin, supports urination, lowers cholesterol. Helps to fight stomach pressure, belching, diabetes, acute or chronic constipation of the intestine. Improves the flow characteristics of the blood.
Cooking time approx. 20 min
Calories p. portion: 254

2 portions
Allergens: G

Quantity of ingredients:
Potato 3/4 lbs / 300g. (yes)
Salt 1 pinch / 0,1g. (little)
Wild garlic (garlic spinach) 2 handful / 30g. (yes)
Curd cheese 20% 5/8 lbs - 8oz / 250g. (recommended)
Yogurt (natural, 1.5% fat) 2 table spoons / 20g. (recommended)
Salt 1 pinch / 1g. (little)

Cooking instructions:
Cook potatoes in salted water and peel.
Wash he wild garlic leaves and carefully dried and cut into fine strips.
Mix the cottage cheese, yogurt and salt and mix in the chopped wild
garlic pieces. Serve with the potatoes.
In the season in which no wild garlic grows the wild garlic pesto can be
used.

9.70 Quick zucchini soup

Diuretic, supports urination. Strengthens gastrointestinal function,
expands blood vessels, prevents cancer, prevents diseases (in the
elderly). Stimulates liver function, detoxifying.
Cooking time approx. 10 min
Calories p. portion: 42
4 portions
Allergens:

Quantity of ingredients:
Zucchini 2-3 pieces / 500g. (recommended)
Onion white 1 piece / 50g. (little)
Corn germ oil 2 table spoons / 6g. (recommended)
Parsley 1 table spoon / 7g. (yes)
Chives 1 teaspoon / 3g. (yes)
Water 2 cup / 400g. (yes)

Cooking instructions:
Fry chopped onion in oil. Add sliced zucchini and sauté well. Pour with
water. Chop parsley and chives, add and puree everything.

9.71 Refreshing cucumber soup with potatoes

Diuretic, detoxifying, suppresses conversion of sugar into fat, lowers cholesterol, prevents cancer, reduces inflammation, improves digestion, lowers cholesterol, dissolves stagnation, improves blood circulation, stimulates appetite.
Cooking time approx. 15 min
Calories p. portion: 148
3 portions
Allergens: GN

Quantity of ingredients:
Sesame oil 1 table spoon / 10g. (recommended)
Potato 4 pieces / 300g. (yes)
Onion (spring onion) 3 pieces / 60g. (little)
Pepper (ground) 1 pinch / 0,5g. (yes)
Nutmeg 1 pinch / 1g. (yes)
Salt 1 pinch / 1g. (little)
Lemon 1/2 piece / 25g. (little)
Cucumber 2 pieces / 500g. (recommended)
Cream, sweet 30% 1 table spoon / 10g. (little)
Dill 1 table spoon / 15g. (yes)

Cooking instructions:
Sauté sesame oil, chopped potatoes, plenty of spring onions in a hot pot; add pepper, a little nutmeg, salt, lemon juice, hot water, diced cucumber; simmer for about 10 minutes and then puree; add some sweet cream as you like, fresh dill.

Variation: Add a little chili, oregano, thyme or rosemary to soften the cooling effect.

9.72 Ribbon noodles with leaf spinach

Promotes digestion, improves blood circulation, forcing spleen and intestine, improves pancreatic function, good to fight loss of appetite, flatulence, inflammatory bowel disease, obesity, stomach ulcers, stomach cramps, rheumatism, heartburn, twelffinger intestinal ulcers.
Cooking time approx. 45 min
Calories p. portion: 722
2 portions
Allergens: ACG

Quantity of ingredients:
Spinach 5/8 lbs - 8oz / 250g. (yes)
Salt 1 pinch / 1g. (little)
Noodles (wheat, ribbon noodles) with egg 5/8 oz / 200g. (yes)
Olive oil 1 table spoon / 15g. (yes)
Onion (spring onion) 1 piece / 20g. (little)
Cream, sweet 30% 1/2 cup / 100g. (little)
Créme fraiche cheese 1/2 teaspoon / 6g. (yes)
Thyme dried 1/2 teaspoon / 2g. (yes)
Basil (fresh) 1/2 teaspoon / 2g. (yes)
Oregano dried 1/2 teaspoon / 2g. (yes)
Nutmeg 1 pinch / 0,5g. (yes)
Pepper (ground) 1 pinch / 0,5g. (yes)
Parmesan 1/2 oz / 20g. (yes)
Pine nuts 1 table spoon / 15g. (yes)
Black caraway 1 pinch / 1g. (yes)

Cooking instructions:
Put the dripping wet spinach together with a little salt for 3 minutes ina pot, then drain in a sieve. Then finely cut.

Boil tagliatelle in plenty of salted water.

Heat the oil in a skillet and fry the spring onions rings. Add cream, crème fraiche, thyme, basil, oregano and nutmeg. Stir in the sauce while stirring. Add the spinach, heat briefly, season with nutmeg, salt and pepper.
Drain pasta and mix with the spinach. Season with salt and pepper. Portion noodles and serve with parmesan and pine nuts. Sprinkle the black cumin over it.

9.73 Rice congee with chicken liver and buckthorn fruit

Good to fight blood circulation disorders, thrombose, risk of embolism, high blood pressure, a headache, heart attack and stroke. Has many vitamins and minerals, high quality amino acid profile. Regulates the blood pressure and blood glucose level, forcing spleen.
Cooking time approx. 3 hours
Calories p. portion: 176
3 portions
Allergens: EO

Quantity of ingredients:
Basic recipe for a rice soup (Congee) 5 cups / 800g. (yes)
Chicken liver 1/2 cup / 60g. (little)
Bocksdorn fruits (Fructus Lycii, Goji, goji berry dried 1/2 cup / 60g. (yes)
Soy sauce 1 dash / 3g. (yes)

Cooking instructions:
Cook basic recipe for rice congee with the chicken liver and berry's; Season with soy sauce.

9.74 Rice pesto with pine nuts

Worming spleen and stomach, harmonizes the intestine.
Cooking time approx. 30 min
Calories p. portion: 274
4 portions
Allergens:

Quantity of ingredients:
Rice variety any 1 1/2 cups / 200g. (yes)
Water 4 cup / 950g. (yes)
Garlic 4 big cloves / 8g. (yes)
Basil Handful / 15g. (yes)
Pine nuts 2 table spoons / 30g. (yes)
Olive oil 2 table spoons / 20g. (yes)

Cooking instructions:
Boil the rice with 1 liter of water. Finely crush the peeled garlic in a mortar or puree with a hand mixer. Add finely crushed basil leaves, then purée the pine nuts a little coarser. Lastly, gradually add the oil until a thick paste forms.
Mix the pesto sauce with the finished rice.

9.75 Roasted barley patties

Improves digestion, lowers cholesterol, good to fight diarrhea, ulceration, joint pain, stomach problems. Promotes spleen and liver, reduces blood pressure, strengthens immune system, prevents cancer, reduces radiation damage, stimulates liver function.
Cooking time approx. 1 1/2 hours
Calories p. portion: 398
3 portions
Allergens: ACN

Quantity of ingredients:
Water 1 1/2 cups / 250g. (yes)
Barley grouts 1 cup / 120g. (yes)
Potato 1 piece / 140g. (yes)
Carrot 1 piece / 120g. (recommended)
Champignon 2-3 pieces / 25g. (yes)
Chicken egg 1 piece / 55g. (yes)
Onion white 1 piece / 50g. (little)
Ginger fresh 1/2 teaspoon / 1g. (yes)
Pepper (ground) 1 pinch / 0,5g. (yes)
Salt 1 pinch / 1g. (little)
Lemon 1/2 piece / 15g. (little)
Parsley 2 table spoons / 15g. (yes)
Peppers powder 1 pinch / 1g. (yes)
Sesame oil 2 table spoons / 50g. (recommended)
Bread roll 1 piece / 35g. (little)

Cooking instructions:
Preparation:
Place 2 large cups of hot water in a saucepan; add 1 large cup of barley porridge; simmer for 2 minutes while stirring; then let it swell for 20 minutes on the switched off stove; take down and let cool.

Cook in boiling water 1 large potato, chopped and cut.

Soak 1 roll in hot water and squeeze well.

Then: Mix the barley groats and crushed the potato. Add 1 grated carrot, 2 - 3 chopped mushrooms, 1 egg, 1 finely chopped onion, 1/2 teaspoon grated ginger, a pinch of pepper, a pinch of salt, a little lemon juice, chopped parsley, plenty of rose paprika; knead well and form patties; heat sesame oil in a hot pan; fry the patties for about 15 minutes over a gentle heat; turn at half time.

Also fits well: lettuce, soybean vegetables.

9.76 Roasted millet with Celery sticks

Promotes spleen and kidney, diuretic, promoting metabolism.
Cooking time approx. 30 min
Calories p. portion: 400
2 portions
Allergens: L

Quantity of ingredients:
Millet 1 cup / 120g. (yes)
Water 1 1/2 cups / 240g. (yes)
Celery sticks 2 rods / 50g. (recommended)
Herbs various 1 table spoon / 10g. (yes)
Water 2 table spoons / 30g. (yes)
Salt 1 pinch / 1g. (little)
Sage 3-4 leaves / 2g. (yes)
Cress 1 teaspoon / 3g. (yes)

Cooking instructions:
Roast millet briefly, pour over water, heat till it boils and let stand for 20 min. to swell.

Cut celery into small pieces and mix with water, salt and fresh herbs and cook for 10 min. Add to the millet.
Sprinkle fresh sage or watercress over it.

9.77 Rosemary Potatoes

Reduces Inflammation, improves digestion, regenerates skin, supports urination, lowers cholesterol. Rosemary stimulates digestion, strengthens lung, promotes spleen and kidney, dries out.
Cooking time approx. 30 min
Calories p. portion: 188
2 portions
Allergens:

Quantity of ingredients:
Potato 6-8 pieces / 420g. (yes)
Salt (herbal) 1 pinch / 1g. (yes)
Olive oil 1 table spoon / 10g. (yes)
Rosemary 1 teaspoon / 2g. (yes)

Cooking instructions:
Cut the potatoes into half´s, apply a little olive oil on the cut surface, then salt, sprinkle 2 - 3 rosemary needles on the potatoes.
Place the potatoes on the baking tray and bake them in the preheated oven for approx. 25 minutes to 190°C/374°F.

9.78 Russian kasha with white cabbage

Promotes digestion, relieves pain, detoxifying, promotes digestion, stimulates appetite, dissolves stagnation, stimulates blood production and metabolism, reduces fat.
Cooking time approx. 30 min
Calories p. portion: 250
2 portions
Allergens: AG

Quantity of ingredients:
Buckwheat whole grain 1 cup / 130g. (yes)
Water 1 1/2 cups / 240g. (yes)
Nutmeg 1 pinch / 1g. (yes)
Salt 1 pinch / 1g. (little)
Parsley 1 table spoon / 10g. (yes)
Ground 1 pinch / 2g. (yes)
Butter organic 1 teaspoon / 3g. (yes)
White cabbage Handful / 20g. (recommended)

Cooking instructions:
Roast buckwheat golden yellow; add boiling water, heat till it boils briefly and then let it swell until soft; Grate the white cabbage finely and fold in. Season with nutmeg, a little salt; some parsley, cumin and butter at the end.

9.79 Salmon on tomato-spinach

Promotes bowel movement, improves blood circulation, forcing spleen and bowel, strengthens blood, reduces inflammation, improves digestion, regenerates skin, supports urination, lowers cholesterol, promotes sweating, dissolves stagnation.
Cooking time approx. 1 hour
Calories p. portion: 365
6 portions
Allergens: D

Quantity of ingredients:
Potato 1,1 lbs / 500g. (yes)
Salt 1 pinch / 1g. (little)
Salmon 1,3 lbs / 600g. (recommended)
Rapeseed oil 2 teaspoons / 24g. (recommended)
Tomato 1/4 lbs - 4oz / 100g. (recommended)
Spinach 1,5 lbs / 700g. (yes)
Salt 1 pinch / 1g. (little)
Pine nuts 4 table spoons / 40g. (yes)
Leek 1/4 lbs - 4oz / 120g. (yes)
Olive oil 4 table spoons / 40g. (yes)
Salt 1 pinch / 1g. (little)
Pepper white (ground) 1 pinch / 0,5g. (yes)

Cooking instructions:
Peel the potato and cut into cubes, cook in salted water.
Cut the salmon into portions and fry slowly and evenly in a frying pan
from both sides, seasoned with salt and pepper, then add the pine nuts
and lightly roast.
Blanch spinach in salted water.
Lightly sweat the finely chopped leek with a little rapeseed oil, add the
blanched spinach and heat evenly.
Just before serving, add the halved cocktail tomatoes to the spinach
and season the vegetables well with salt and pepper.
Arrange the spinach and leek tomato bed with the potatoes, add the
salmon and sprinkle with the salted pine nuts.

Drizzle with a little olive oil and serve the dish.

9.80 Semolina soup with vegetables

Reduces blood pressure, strengthens immune system, prevents cancer,
forcing spleen, dissolves stagnation, promotes weight loss. Good to
fight immunodeficiency, loss of appetite, flatulence, high blood
pressure, depressions, diabetes, diarrhea, rheumatism, heartburn,
twelffinger intestinal ulcers.
Cooking time approx. 20 min
Calories p. portion: 105
3 portions
Allergens: AGL

Quantity of ingredients:
Basic recipe for a vegetable soup (nutritious) 2 cup / 500g. (yes)
Wheat semolina 2 table spoons / 20g. (yes)
Lovage 1/2 teaspoon / 2g. (yes)
Basil (fresh) 1/2 teaspoon / 1g. (yes)
Nutmeg 1 pinch / 0,1g. (yes)
Carrot 1/4 lbs - 4oz / 100g. (recommended)
Celery root 1/8 lbs - 2oz / 50g. (recommended)
Cream, sweet 30% 2 table spoons / 30g. (little)
Parsley 1 table spoon / 10g. (yes)

Cooking instructions:
Roast wheat grits without fat in a pan. Roast the chopped carrots and celery briefly. Add the vegetable soup (Basic recipe for a vegetable soup). Season with lovage, nutmeg and let it 10 min. simmer.
Stir in the cream before serving and garnish with parsley.

9.81 Sliced lamb with rosemary potatoes

Improves digestion, regenerates skin, supports urination, lowers cholesterol, strengthens immune system, expands blood vessels.
Cooking time approx. 1 hour
Calories p. portion: 461
4 portions
Allergens: LO

Quantity of ingredients:
Lamb meat 7/8 lbs - 1 lbs / 500g. (yes)
Olive oil 2 table spoons / 20g. (yes)
Onion white 1 piece / 50g. (little)
Garlic 1 clove / 2g. (yes)
Nutmeg 1 pinch / 0,2g. (yes)
Carrot 3 pieces / 150g. (recommended)
Celery root 1/4 tuber / 120g. (recommended)
Rosemary 1 Twig / 3g. (yes)
Savory 1 teaspoon / 2g. (recommended)
Parsley 1 table spoon / 8g. (yes)
Pepper powder (hot) 1 pinch / 2g. (yes)
Red wine 1/2 cup / 125g. (little)
Salt (herbal) 1 pinch / 1g. (yes)
Lemon juice 1/2 piece / 15g. (little)
Cranberry 1 table spoon / 10g. (recommended)
Potato 6 pieces / 400g. (yes)

Cooking instructions:
Cut the lamb into strips, cut the carrots and celery into small cubes.

Heat the olive oil in a pan, fry the lamb in it, add the cut onions and garlic, salt with herbal salt, a little water, parsley, deglaze with red wine, season with paprika and small cut rosemary, mugwort, savory, carrots and celery, turn the heat back on small Simmer for about 35 minutes. Season with pepper and nutmeg, if necessary still salt, add a little lemon juice, season with paprika, cranberries.

Cut the potatoes in half, the length of, spread a little olive oil on the cut surface, salt, sprinkle 2-3 rosemary needles on each half potato, place the potatoes on the baking sheet and bake in a preheated oven for approx. 25 minutes at 190°C/374°F.

9.82 Spinach with Tahini

Promotes bowel movement, improves blood circulation, forcing spleen and bowel, improves pancreatic function. Improves digestion, regenerates skin, supports urination, lowers cholesterol. Gentle laxative.
Cooking time approx. 20 min
Calories p. portion: 150
4 portions
Allergens: N

Quantity of ingredients:
Potato 1,1 lbs / 500g. (yes)
Salt 1 pinch / 0,2g. (little)
Water 1 cup / 25g. (yes)
Spinach 2,2 lbs / 800g. (yes)
Sesame paste (Tahini) 2 table spoons / 20g. (yes)

Cooking instructions:
Cook potatoes and peel. Heat water. Blanch spinach. Shake off water and let it dry and stir with sesame.

9.83 Spring salad

Blood-forming, blood detoxifying, diuretic, good to fight stomach discomfort, improves digestion, diarrhea, helps to digest fat, supports urination, reduces blood pressure, detoxifying, reduces inflammation, diuretic.
Cooking time approx. 10 min
Calories p. portion: 162
4 portions
Allergens: AEMN

Quantity of ingredients:
Sorrel 3/8 lbs - 6oz / 6oz / 150g. (yes)
Dandelion (young plants) 1/4 lbs - 4oz / 100g. (yes)
Mung bean sprouting 0,2 lbs / 75g. (yes)
Cress 1/4 lbs - 4oz / 100g. (yes)
Chives 1 Bunch / 50g. (yes)
Tomato 2 pieces / 100g. (recommended)
Parsley 1 Bunch / 50g. (yes)
Sesame paste (Tahini) 2 table spoons / 16g. (yes)
Soy sauce 1 dash / 3g. (yes)
Mustard 1/2 teaspoon / 2g. (yes)
White bread (wheat bread) 6 slices / 120g. (little)

Cooking instructions:
Wash all salad´s, mix and prepare the sauce as follows:
Mix tahini with mustard and balsamic vinegar, tamari, olive oil, chives and half of parsley. Pour the sauce over the salad and sprinkle the remaining parsley just before serving.
Serve with the white bread.

9.84 Stew with sweet potato and leeks

Strengthens muscles, tendons and bones, reduces blood pressure, strengthens immune system, reduces fat, improves digestion. Promotes sweating, dissolves stagnation, stimulates appetite and digestion.
Cooking time approx. 30 min
Calories p. portion: 316
2 portions
Allergens: GO

Quantity of ingredients:
Sweet potato 5/8 oz / 200g. (yes)
Leek 1/8 lbs - 2oz / 50g. (yes)
Butter organic 2 table spoons / 20g. (yes)
Nutmeg 1 pinch / 0,1g. (yes)
Basic recipe for a beef soup (warming) 2 cup / 480g. (yes)
Salt 1 pinch / 1g. (little)
Curcuma 1 pinch / 0,5g. (yes)
Herbs various 1 pinch of fresh / 1g. (yes)
Black caraway 1 pinch / 1g. (yes)

Cooking instructions:
Peel potatoes, cut into coarse cubes and cook (not too soft) in salted water, drain. Heat the butter in a saucepan and sauté the leek. Add the soup and add the leek and the sweet potato. Season with nutmeg, turmeric, fresh herbs, crushed black cumin and salt.

9.85 Sweet potato pancakes with basil pesto

Strengthens the immune system, reduces fat, Improves digestion, calms nerves and stomach, dissolves stones, improves blood circulation, strengthens the muscles, antioxidativ.
Cooking time approx. 30 min
Calories p. portion: 625
3 portions
Allergens: ACH

Quantity of ingredients:
Sweet potato 4 pieces / 500g. (yes)
Onion read 1/2 piece / 30g. (little)
Basil 1 table spoon / 10g. (yes)
Chicken egg 2 pieces / 140g. (yes)
Spelled wholemeal flour 3 oz / 80g. (yes)
Salt 1 pinch / 0,5g. (little)
Olive oil 1/4 cup / 20g. (yes)
Salt 1 teaspoon (coarse) / 3g. (little)
Basil Handful / 15g. (yes)
Parsley Handful / 15g. (yes)
Garlic 2 cloves / 3g. (yes)
Walnuts 1/8 lbs - 2oz / 60g. (recommended)
Olive oil 2 table spoons / 20g. (yes)

Cooking instructions:
Sweet Potato Buffer: Wash the sweet potato thoroughly, but do not peel, and grate into a large bowl. Add onion, basil, egg and flour, mix well and sprinkle with salt. The mixture can be formed into buffers. Bake in a preheated tube on a baking tray coated with oil for 4 to 5 minutes on both sides.

Basil Pesto: Add the salt, chopped basil and parsley and crushed garlic in a small bowl and crush (if available, use the mortar). Add the grated walnuts. While stirring, add enough olive oil until the desired consistency is achieved.

9.86 Tea from basil

Good to fight bloating and nausea, relaxing and reassuring.
Cooking time approx. 10 min
Calories p. portion: 0
4 portions
Allergens:

Quantity of ingredients:
Basil 1 teaspoon / 2g. (yes)
Water 2 cup / 500g. (yes)

Cooking instructions:
Heat the water till it boils and put it aside. Add basil and 10 min. to let go. Sweet to taste with honey.

9.87 Tea from chamomile

Good to fight flatulence, nausea, intestinal cramps, diarrhea, inflammation of the oral mucosa, influenza infections, stomach and intestinal mucosa infections, badly healing wounds, nausea, colds, skin rashes, inflammation in the genital and anal area.
Cooking time approx. 10 min
Calories p. portion: 0
1 portions
Allergens:

Quantity of ingredients:
Chamomile 1 teaspoon / 3g. (yes)
Water 1 cup / 120g. (yes)

Cooking instructions:
Heat the water till it boils and put it aside. Chamomile flowers added and 10 min. to let go.

9.88 Tea from lime blossom

The sweating effect can be used in feverish colds. The lime blossom tea activates the body's defenses, which helps to overcome the colds associated with fever more quickly.
Cooking time approx. 10 min
Calories p. portion: 0
2 portions
Allergens:

Quantity of ingredients:
Lime blossom tea 1 teabag / 2g. (yes)
Water 2 cup / 500g. (yes)

Cooking instructions:
Heat the water till it boils and put it aside. Add the linden blossoms and leave for 10 min. to let go. Sweet to taste with honey. Strain when pouring.

9.89 Tea from mallow

Relieves irritation cough, soothes mucous membranes in mouth, throat, stomach and intestines, inhibits inflammation, easily contracting (astringent).
Cooking time approx. 10 min
Calories p. portion: 0
4 portions
Allergens:

Quantity of ingredients:
Mallow (Malva sylvestris) blossom tea 2 teabags / 4g. (yes)
Water 2 cup / 500g. (yes)

Cooking instructions:
Heat the water till it boils and put it aside. Add mallow tee and 10 min. to let go. Sweet to taste with honey. Strain when pouring.

9.90 Tea Green tea

Green tea promotes digestion, supports urination, dissolves mucus, detoxifying, stimulates nerves, reduces blood lipids, lowers cholesterol, reduces inflammation.
Cooking time approx. 10 min
Calories p. portion: 2
1 portions
Allergens:

Quantity of ingredients:
Green tea 1 teaspoon / 2g. (yes)
Water 1 cup / 120g. (yes)

Cooking instructions:
For each cup you use a teaspoonful or a teabag.
Pour green tea only with 60 to 80 ° C / 140 to 176 °F hot water, otherwise it will be bitter.
If the tea has a stimulating effect, let it draw for two to three minutes. It has a calming effect for a duration of five minutes (no longer, otherwise it will be bitter!).
Another method: Pour the tea leaves with about 70 ° C / 158 °F hot water and pour the water immediately again.
Then just pour hot water again. The bitter substances disappear and the tea gets a milder aroma.

9.91 Tofu-Black Bean Chili with Rice

Supports urination, lowers cholesterol, prevents arteriosclerosis, for the drainage of the body overweight and high blood pressure, strengthens immune system.
Cooking time approx. 45 min
Calories p. portion: 344
4 portions
Allergens: AEL

Quantity of ingredients:
Rapeseed oil 1/4 cup / 60g. (recommended)
Onion white 2 pieces / 120g. (little)
Peppers 1 piece / 20g. (recommended)
Pepper Cayenne 1 pinch / 0,5g. (yes)
Coriander 1 teaspoon / 2g. (yes)
Thyme 1 teaspoon / 2g. (yes)
Clove 1 teaspoon / 2g. (yes)

Spelled wholemeal flour 2 table spoons / 16g. (yes)
Sherry (whine) 1 table spoon / 8g. (little)
Soy Tofu 5/8 lbs - 8oz / 250g. (yes)
Black beans 2 cans (400g) / 400g. (yes)
Basic recipe for a chicken soup (warming) 1 1/2 cups / 300g. (yes)
Bay leaf 1 piece / 0,2g. (yes)
Garlic 6 pieces / 8g. (yes)
Water 6 cups / 400g. (yes)
Rice Basmati 1 cup / 120g. (yes)

Cooking instructions:
Heat the oil at medium temperature in a large saucepan, add onions,
paprika and chili powder and fry for 2 minutes until the onions are
glassy.
Add the remaining spices, stirring constantly, stirring until the aroma
rises.
Dust the flour, fry for 2 minutes and make sure that the paste-like spice
mixture does not burn.
Deglaze with sherry, add the black beans (tin) and mix with the spices.
Add the chicken broth, add the bay leaf and stir in the chopped garlic.
Simmer the beans for 30 minutes and add some chicken stock if
needed.
Cook the tofu cubes during the last 10 minutes. The tofu can easily
disintegrate and should therefore be lifted very gently with a wooden
spoon.
Finally, pick out the bay leaf and serve the tofu black bean chili with
rice.

9.92 Turkey breast with vegetables (Asian)

Strengthens blood, strengthens bone marrow, dissolves stagnation,
promotes digestion and is goo to fight high blood pressure. Rice to drain
the body at overweight and high blood pressure.
Cooking time approx. 45 min
Calories p. portion: 535
2 portions
Allergens: AEN

Quantity of ingredients:
Rice variety any 1 cup / 120g. (yes)
Water 6 cups / 240g. (yes)
Turkey breast meat 5/8 oz / 200g. (recommended)
Ginger fresh 1/3 inch / 3g. (yes)

Garlic 1 piece / 2g. (yes)
Soy sauce 2 table spoons / 20g. (yes)
Wheat flour 2 teaspoons / 15g. (yes)
Onion (spring onion) 2 pieces / 40g. (little)
Peppers 1/2 piece / 10g. (recommended)
Champignon 8 pieces / 30g. (yes)
Sesame oil 2 table spoons / 20g. (recommended)
Soy sauce 1 table spoon / 12g. (yes)
Curry 1 pinch / 2g. (yes)
Turmeric (yellow root) 1 pinch / 2g. (yes)
Cashews 2 teaspoons / 25g. (yes)

Cooking instructions:
Cook the rice in salted water.
Cut the turkey meat into thin strips. Peel and dice the ginger and garlic. Put together with the meat strips in a bowl.
Mix 1 tbsp of soy sauce with the wheat starch and stir until smooth. Add to the meat and marinate for 30 minutes.
Wash spring onions and peppers, clean and cut into small pieces.
Clean and quarter the mushrooms.
Put one tablespoon of sesame oil in a pan and sauté and warm the marinated turkey. Now add the remaining oil to the pan and fry the other vegetables in it. Now add the meat and season with soy sauce and spices. Serve with the rice. Sprinkle the cashews over the dish before serving.

9.93 Vegetable bowl with tofu and curry on rice

Diuretic, reduces blood glucose. Reduces flatulence, supports digestion. Contains ideal herbal mucus, which provides regeneration of the small and large intestinal flora. Reduces blood pressure, strengthens immune system.
Cooking time approx. 30 min
Calories p. portion: 162
6 portions
Allergens: E

Quantity of ingredients:
Olive oil 2 table spoons / 20g. (yes)
Garlic 2 cloves / 3g. (yes)
Onion white 1 piece / 60g. (little)
Curry 2 table spoons / 16g. (yes)
Water 2 cup / 500g. (yes)

Turnips 2 pieces / 50g. (recommended)
Pumpkin 1 piece / 400g. (yes)
Carrot 1 piece / 100g. (recommended)
Parsnip 1 piece / 150g. (yes)
Potato 1 piece / 70g. (yes)
Sweet potato 1 piece / 70g. (yes)
Cauliflower 1/4 piece / 250g. (recommended)
Broccoli 1/2 piece / 250g. (recommended)
Okra 12 pieces / 200g. (yes)
Soy Tofu 1 piece / 250g. (yes)
Basil 2 table spoons / 12g. (yes)
Salt 1 pinch / 0,5g. (little)

Cooking instructions:
Heat the oil at medium temperature in a large, heavy casserole, add the garlic and onion and sauté with constant stirring. Sprinkle curry powder over it, fry gently for about 5 minutes and make sure that the garlic and curry do not burn. Add the water and heat till it boils. Gradually peel all vegetables, dice and add, starting with the varieties that need the longest cooking time. Once the water has boiled again, reduce the heat and simmer the vegetables for about 15 minutes. When it is almost soft. Add the cauliflower and broccoli florets and the okra and cook the stew for another 10 to 15 minutes. Add the tofu during the last 5 minutes.

Cook the brown rice at the same time: Sprinkle the rice in a medium saucepan with water, salt and cover for about 20 minutes. cook on a low heat. Take from the fire and another 10 min. to let go.

Arrange the stew over the brown rice and sprinkle with basil.

9.94 Vegetable miso soup with tofu

Very powerful, strengthens after febrile illness, reduces blood pressure, strengthens immune system, prevents cancer, reduces radiation damage, improves blood circulation, strengthens liver and kidney, detoxifying, strengthens the muscles, reduces flatulence, forcing spleen.
Cooking time approx. 15 min
Calories p. portion: 107
4 portions
Allergens: EN

Quantity of ingredients:
Sesame oil 2 table spoons / 35g. (recommended)
Onion (shallot) 1 piece / 20g. (little)
Carrot 1 piece / 70g. (recommended)
Leek 2 inches / 10g. (yes)
Water 3 cups / 750g. (yes)
Endive salad 2 table spoons / 30g. (yes)
Soy Tofu 2 table spoons / 30g. (yes)
Ginger fresh 1/2 teaspoon / 1g. (yes)
Miso 2 table spoons / 15g. (yes)

Cooking instructions:
In sesame oil first sauté onions, then carrots and a little leek; Pour in water and simmer gently; add the bean sprouts and endive leaves and leave to stand; Tofu cubes, add a little ginger; at the end stir in a little cooled cooking-water the Miso.

9.95 Vegetable rice

Forcing spleen, dissolves stagnation, promotes weight loss. Good to fight immunodeficiency, loss of appetite, flatulence, high blood pressure, strengthens kidney and bladder. Diuretic, warming the body from the inside, regulates internal organs functions.
Cooking time approx. 30 min
Calories p. portion: 304
3 portions
Allergens: L

Quantity of ingredients:
Broccoli 1/8 lbs - 2oz / 50g. (recommended)
Carrot 1/8 lbs - 2oz / 50g. (recommended)
Kohlrabi 1/8 lbs - 2oz / 50g. (recommended)
Cauliflower 1 oz / 30g. (recommended)
Peas 1/2 oz / 20g. (yes)
Margarine 1 teaspoon / 4g. (yes)
Rice (whole grain) 5/8 oz / 200g. (recommended)
Basic recipe for a vegetable soup (nutritious) 7/8 lbs / 400g. (yes)
Parsley 1/2 oz / 20g. (yes)
Pepper (ground) 1 pinch / 0,2g. (yes)

Cooking instructions:
Cut the broccoli, carrots and kohlrabi into small cubes, divide the cauliflower into small florets. Heat the margarine in a pan or saucepan, sauté the vegetables. Then add the rice, top up with the vegetable stock and leave to soak for 15-20 minutes.

In the meantime finely chop the parsley. After cooking, season the rice with freshly ground pepper and parsley.

9.96 Yellow lentil soup

Strengthens heart and kidney, diuretic, promotes spleen, calms the stomach, promotes digestion, strengthens immune system, prevents cancer, reduces radiation damage, stimulates liver function, antioxidativ.
Cooking time approx. 20 min
Calories p. portion: 155
7 portions
Allergens: A

Quantity of ingredients:
Lentils yellow 1 lbs / 500g. (yes)
Carrot 2 pieces / 150g. (recommended)
Kohlrabi 1 piece / 300g. (recommended)
Onion white 1 piece / 50g. (little)
Parsley 1/2 bunch / 100g. (yes)
Turmeric (yellow root) 1 pinch / 1g. (yes)
Cardamom 1 pinch / 1g. (yes)
Salt 1 pinch / 1g. (little)
Olive oil 1 table spoon / 10g. (yes)
Water 4 cup / 1000g. (yes)
Lemon juice 1/2 piece / 15g. (little)
White bread (wheat bread) 7 slices / 140g. (little)

Cooking instructions:
Wash lenses well in a colander. Heat oil in a pot. Add finely chopped onion, sliced carrots, diced kohlrabi and spices, sauté and salt. Add the lentils and cover with water and simmer for 20 minutes. Add water as needed and season with salt. Sprinkle with fresh parsley or fresh green cilantro and drizzle with lemon juice.
Here you can also use red lenses. (same cooking time).
Serve with white bread.

9.97 Zucchini with basil pesto

Good to fight bloating and nausea. Relaxing and reassuring, promotes digestion, forcing spleen and digestive system, detoxifying, strengthens the muscles and bones, diuretic, supports urination, dissolves stagnation.
Cooking time approx. 25 min
Calories p. portion: 468
3 portions
Allergens: ACGHL

Quantity of ingredients:
Basil (fresh) 1 Bunch / 125g. (yes)
Olive oil 1 table spoon / 20g. (yes)
Almond 1 table spoon / 15g. (yes)
Parmesan 1 oz / 30g. (yes)
Basic recipe for a vegetable soup (nutritious) 2 table spoons / 45g. (yes)
Lemon peel 1 teaspoon / 3g. (little)
Lemon 1 teaspoon / 3g. (little)
Oregano dried 2 teaspoons / 15g. (yes)
Ground 1 pinch / 1g. (yes)
Salt 1 pinch / 1g. (little)
Pepper (ground) 1 pinch / 1g. (yes)
Noodles (wheat, spaghetti) with egg 5/8 oz / 200g. (yes)
Salt 1 pinch / 1g. (little)
Olive oil 1 table spoon / 15g. (yes)
Onion (spring onion) 2 pieces / 40g. (little)
Zucchini 5/8 lbs - 8oz / 250g. (recommended)

Cooking instructions:
Mix Basil, olive oil, grated almonds, parmesan, vegetable broth and grated lemon peel to a smooth cream puree.
Season the pesto with salt, oregano, cumin and pepper.
Boil the spaghetti with a little salt in plenty of water.
Heat the olive oil in a pan and fry the spring onions while stirring. Add zucchini and fry briefly with stirring. The zucchini should be soft with a bite. Season the zucchini with salt.
In a bowl, mix well-drained spaghetti with zucchini and pesto. Season the spaghetti with salt and pepper.
Recommended for dysphagia, loss of appetite, potassium and magnesium requirements.

10 Effects of food

10.1 Use ingredients: recommendable

Acai powder
Asparagus (green or white)
Beans (green, fresh)
Bitter Herb liqueur
Blackberry´s
Borage
Broccoli
Brussels sprouts
Carrot
Carrot (Early Carrot)
Carrot juice without sugar
Cauliflower
Celery root
Celery sticks
Chicory
Chinese cabbage
Cod
Corn germ oil
Cranberry
Cranberry juice
Cream 10% coffee cream
Cucumber
Cucumber (bitter)
Cucumber (spicy cucumber)
Curd cheese 20%
Currant (black)
Currant (red)
Currant (white)
Fennel
Fish pieces mixed (fresh water)
Fox nut, gorgon nut, makhana
Gourd
Herbal tea mix
Herring
Hibiscus
Juniper berry
Kohlrabi
Kudzu
Lamb's lettuce
Lamb's lettuce
Leaf salads (bitter)
Lentils
Lettuce
Lily bulbs
Linseed oil
Mackerel
Manioc flour
Mascarpone cheese
Mediterranean fish (cod, plaice,

haddock, sea eel, mackerel)
Muesli
Noodles (whole grain) with egg
Oat flakes (whole grain)
Oat fusion (baby food)
Peppers
Plaice
Processed cheese 12%
Radicchio
Radish
Radish (white, green, purple-red)
Radish horseradish
Rapeseed oil
Raspberry
Red beet
Red cabbage
Rhubarb
Rice (whole grain)
Rice mash
Rice wild (nature rice)
Rose hip tea
Rosefish
Rucola
Rye wholemeal bread
Salmon
Savory
Savoy cabbage / kale
Sesame oil
Soya Cuisine (soy cream)
Soybeans
Tomato
Trout
Tuna
Turkey breast meat
Turnip
Turnips
Vegetable juice
Walnuts
Wax gourd
Wheat bran
Wheat flour whole grain
Wheat germ oil
Wheat/Rye/Gray-black bread with yeast
White cabbage
Whole grain bread
Wholemeal flour
Wild herbs
Yogurt (natural, 1.5% fat)
Zucchini

10.2 Use ingredients: yes

Adzuki beans
Agar agar (kelp)
Agave nectar
Agrimony
Almond
Almond marzipan
Almond milk
Almond puree
Aloe juice
Amaranth
Amaranth Pops
Anchovy / Sardine
Angelica root
Anise (Common Fennel)
Arrowroot
Artichoke
Aubergine
Avocado
Baking powder
Balm
Bamboo shoots
Banchatee (green tea)
barberry
Barley
Barley flour
Barley grass powder
Barley grouts
Barley malt
Barley not peeled
Basic recipe for a beef soup
Basic recipe for a beef soup (warming)
Basic recipe for a chicken soup
(warming)
Basic recipe for a duck soup
Basic recipe for a fish soup
Basic recipe for a rice soup (Congee)
Basic recipe for a vegetable soup
(nutritious)
Basil
Basil (fresh)
Batavia
Bay leaf
Bean oil
Bearberry leaf
Beef bone marrow
Beef fillet
Beef heart
Beef heart (calf)
Beef lungs (calf)
Beef meat
Beef meat (calf)

Beef meatbones
Beef Oxtail pieces
Beef soup meat

Beef stomach
Berries of the season
Berry juice
Bitter Lemon
Bitter orange peel
Black beans
Black caraway
Black fungus mushroom
Black tea
Blackberry dried (unripe fruit)
Blackberry jam
Blackberry leaves
Black-eyed peas
Blackthorn (Sloe)
Blue mallow tee
Blueberry
Blueberry dried
Blueberry jam
Bocksdorn fruits (Fructus Lycii, Goji,
goji berry dried
Boletus mushroom
Borage oil
Boxhorn clover seeds
Brazil nuts
Bread with carob kernel flour
Breadcrumbs (wheat bread, bread roll)
Brie cheese
Broad beans (thick beans)
Buckbean
Buckwheat
Buckwheat (roasted) Kasha
Buckwheat whole grain
Bulgur (cereals)
Burdock root tea
Bush beans
Butter (half fat)
Butter beans white
Butter organic
Buttermilk
Calamari
Camembert
Capers in olive oil
Cardamom
Carob flour, St. john's bread
Carp
Cashews
Caviar

Cereal coffee
Chamomile
Chamomile tea
Champignon
Channa-Dal
Chanterelle
Chard
Chenpi (chinese tangerine bowl)
Chervil
Chervil dried
Chestnut puree
Chestnuts
Chicken Blood
Chicken egg
Chicken egg white
Chicken heart
Chicken meat
Chicken stomach
Chickpeas
Chickweed
Chili (pod or ground)
Chinese pearl barley
Chives
Chlorella (fresh water)
Chrysanthemum blossom tea
Cinnamon ground
Cinnamon sticks
Clove
Cocoa
Coconut flakes
Coconut grated
Coconut meat
Coconut milk
Codfish
Coffee
Coix (seeds) YiYi Ren
Cola drink (low calorie)
Cooking oil
Coriander
Coriander (fresh)
Corn
Corn (fast polenta)
Corn (roasted)
Corn flour
Corn Grease (Polenta)
Corn silk tea
Corn starch
Cottage cheese
Couscous
Cow's milk (1.5% fat)
Cow's milk (whole milk 3.5% fat)
Crab
Cranberries
Cranberry

Cranberry jam
Cream sour 10%
Cream sour 20%
Cream sour 30%
Creamer
Créme fraiche cheese
Cress
Crispbread
Crucian
Cumin (Caraway seed)
Curcuma
Curd cheese 40%
Currant jam (black)
Currant jam (red)
Curry
Curry paste red
Daisy
Dandelion (young plants)
Dandelion juice
Dandelionroots tea
Dashi
Deer meat
Deer meat
Deer's Bones
Deer's kidneys
Dill
Duck (heart)
Duck (slaughtered)
Ducks egg
Dulse (seaweed)
Dyer's broom herb
Edam cheese
Eel
Eel smoked
Elderberries
Elderberry blossom tee
Emmental cheese
Endive salad
Evening primrose oil
Fennel seeds ground
Fennel tea
Fenugreek (Trigonella foenum-graecum)
Feta cheese
Feta cheese
Fish sauce
Flounder
Flower pollen
French beans
Fresh cheese
Fresh cheese from soya
Fresh cheese with herbs
Freshwater crab
Freshwater fish

Fructose (glucose)
Fruit mix juice
Fruit tea
Galangal
Garam Masala powder
Garlic
Gelatin white
Gelee Royal
Gentian root
Gentian root tea
Ginger fresh
Ginger oil
Ginger powder
Ginseng
Ginseng root
Goat
Goat and sheep's blood
Goat and sheep's brain
Goat and sheep's milk
Goat and sheep's stomach
Goat cheese
Goose
Goose blood
Goose egg
Goose fat
Goose parts
Gooseberry
Gorgonzola
Gouda cheese
Grapeseed oil
Grass carp
Green spelt
Green tea
Ground
Ground caraway
Guava
Halibut (Flatfish)
Hawthorn
Hazelnuts
Herbs bitter
Herbs of Provence
Herbs various
Herbs wild
Hibiscus tea
Hijiki
Hokkaido pumpkin
Honey
Hop
Horehound leaves
Horse meat
Hyssop
Iceberg lettuce
Jasmine blossoms tee
Jellyfish

Kalmus
Kefir
Kidney beans (red)
King Solomon's-seal
Kombu seaweed (Saccharina japonica)
Kukicha tea
Kumquats
Ladyfingers
Lamb bones
Lamb meat
Lamb shoulder
Lavender blossoms
Leek
Lemon Balm (dried)
Lemon Balm (fresh)
Lemongrass
Lentils black
Lentils red
Lentils yellow
Licorice root tea
Lima beans
Lime blossom tea
Linseed
Linseed (crushed)
Liver smoothing tea
Lobster
Longane
Loquate / Japanese medlar
Lotus roots
Lotus seeds
Lovage
Lovage seeds
Lye roll
Mallow (Malva sylvestris) blossom tea
Malt
Maple syrup
Mare's milk
Margarine
Margarine (diet)
Marjoram
Millet
Millet flakes
Mineral water
Miso
Miso black (fermented)
Miso paste (soy bean paste)
Mixed Pickles
Mold cheese
Morel (black, dried)
Morel, dried
Mozzarella
Mu Erh Mushroom
Mulled Wine Spice
Mullet

Multi-grain bread (gray bread)
Mung bean
Mung bean sprouting
Mussels
Mustard
Mustard Dijon
Mustard medium hot
Mustard seeds
Mustard sweet
Mutton
Mutton
Nasturtium (nose-twister or nose-tweaker)
Nettles
Noodles (wheat) with egg
Noodles (wheat, lasagne) with egg
Noodles (wheat, ribbon noodles) with egg
Noodles (wheat, spaghetti) with egg
Nori, purple seaweed, red algae
Nutmeg
Oat
Oat flakes roasted
Oat flour
Oat meal
Oat milk
Octopus
Octopus
Okra
Olive oil
Olives
Olives green
Orange blossom
Orange peel
Oregano dried
Oregano fresh
Oyster mushroom
Oyster shell powder
Oysters
Palm oil
Parmesan
Parsley
Parsley root
Parsnip
Passion blossoms tea
Peanut butter
Peanut oil
Peanuts
Pearl barley
Pearl barley
Peas
Peas, green
Pepper (ground)
Pepper Cayenne

Pepper powder (hot)
Pepper white (ground)
Peppercorns
Peppermint
Peppermint tea
Pepperoni
Pepperoni, red, pitted, halved
Pepperoni, yellow, pitted, halved
Peppers (rose peppers)
Peppers (sweet)
Peppers powder
Perch
Pheasant
Pickle
Pig blood
Pigeon
Pigeon egg
Pimento
Pine nuts
Pinto beans speckled
Pistachios
Poppy
Pork Bacon
Pork brain
Pork fat (lard)
Pork ham
Pork ham cooked
Pork ham smoked
Pork knuckle
Pork lung
Pork marrow bones
Pork meat
Pork sausage (Bratwurst)
Pork skin
Pork stomach
Pork/beef sausage (smoked)
Pork's intestine
Potato
Potato (mealy)
Potato flour
processed cheese 30%
Psyllium seed
Pudding powder vanilla
Puff pastry
Pumpernickel (dark bread)
Pumpkin
Pumpkin seed oil
Pumpkin seeds
Quail
Quail egg
Quinoa
Rabbit
Rabbit (wild)
Rabbit liver

Rabbit meat
Radish black
Radish leaves
Raspberry dried (immature)
Raspberry jam
Raspberry leaf tea
Reishi mushroom
Ribworttea
Rice (fragrance)
Rice (Gaoliang / Sorghum)
Rice Basmati
Rice black
Rice flour
Rice long grain rice
Rice malt
Rice noodles
Rice red
Rice round grain
Rice starch
Rice sticky
Rice sweet
Rice variety any
Romaine lettuce / lettuce salad
Rose blossom tea
Rose leaf tea
Rosemary
Rusk
Rye
Rye flour
Safflower (Dyer's thistle / Hong Hua)
Saffron
Sage
Sago (cereals)
Sake
Salsify
Salt (herbal)
Sauerkraut (cutted cabbage fermented)
Sea buckthorn
Sea cucumber
Seacrab
Sesame oil roasted
Sesame paste (Tahini)
Sesame, black
Sesame, white
Shark
Sheep's milk
Sheep's milk yoghurt
Shiitake, dried
Shrimp
Shrimps
Skim milk powder
Slug
Sorrel
Sour cream 15% fat

Sour milk
Sour milk cheese 20%
Sourdough
Soy flour
Soy noodles
Soy sauce
Soy Tofu
Soy Tofu smoked
Soybean milk
Soybean oil
Soybeans, black
Soybeans, blacks, fermented
Soybeans, yellow
Spelled (Dark) bread
Spelled flakes
Spelled grain
Spelled semolina
Spelled wholemeal flour
Spinach
Spiny lobsters
Spurdog (spiny dogfish, Schillerlocken)
St. Benedict's thistle, blessed thistle,
holy thistle, spotted thistle
Star anise
Stevia (candyleaf, sweetleaf)
Sugar Milk Sugar
Sugar substitute (sweetener)
Sunflower oil
Sunflower seeds
Sweet potato
Tabasco
Tarragon (Estragon)
Tea mixture uric acid lowering
Thistle oil
Thyme
Thyme dried
Toast bread (whole grain)
Tomato dried
Tomato juice
Tomato paste
Tomato puree
Tonic Water
Topinambur
Trout (smoked)
Truffle
Tsampa (roasted barley flour)
Turkey ham
Turmeric (yellow root)
Umeboshi paste
Umeboshi plums (Japanese apricots)
Valerian
Vanilla
Vanilla pod
Vanilla powder

Vanilla sugar natural
Vinegar (Apple vinegar)
Vinegar (Red wine vinegar)
Vinegar Aceto Balsamico
Vinegar Aceto Balsamico white
Wakame
Walnut oil
Walnuts roasted
Water
Water hot
Wheat
Wheat bulgur
Wheat flakes
Wheat flatbread/pita bread
Wheat flour
Wheat semolina
Wheat semolina for children

Wheatgrass juice
Wheatgrass powder
Whey
White beans
Whitefish
Wild boar meat
Wild garlic (garlic spinach)
Wild strawberries
Wormwood herb
Yam root, yam root tuber
Yarrow
Yarrow tea
Yeast
Yew nut
Yoghurt vanilla
Yogi tea
Yogurt (natural, 3.5% fat)

10.3 Use ingredients: little

Beef kidney
Beef liver
Beer (alcohol-free)
Beer (alcohol-reduced)
Beer (Pils)
Beer (Top-fermented German dark beer)
Bitter liqueur
Bread roll
Brown ale
Campari
Chicken liver
Chicken yolk
Chocolate
Chocolate (Diabetic)
Clarified butter
Coconut fat
Cola drink
Cream (30% fat)
Cream, sweet 30%
Fernet Branca (herbal bitter liqueur)
Fish innards
Fish remains
Ginseng liqueur
Goat and sheep's liver
Grapefruit dried peel
Honey wine (Met)
Lamb kidneys
Lamb liver
Lemon
Lemon juice
Lemon peel
Lychee liqueur

Martini
Mayonnaise 50%
Mayonnaise 80%
Onion (shallot)
Onion (spring onion)
Onion read
Onion white
Orange grated peel
Peanut (roasted)
Pork heart
Pork kidneys
Pork Lard
Pork liver
Prosecco
Red wine
Rum
Salt
Sherry (whine)
Spirit
Sugar - icing sugar
Sugar brown
Sugar candy white
Sugar cane sugar
Sugar molasses
Sugar palm sugar
Sugar white
Wheat beer
White bread (baguette)
White bread (pretzel sticks)
White bread (roll)
White bread (wheat bread)
White breadcrumbs
White dumpling bread (wheat bread cut

into chunks)
White wine

Wormwood

10.4 Do not use contra-acting foods

Acerola fruit nectar or powder
Apple (sour)
Apple (sweet)
Apple juice (natural cloudy)
Apple puree
Apricot
Apricot dried
Apricot jam
Apricot nectar
Apricots
Apricots juice
Banana
Banana (cooking banana)
Blueberry juice
Cantaloupe
Carambola (Star fruit)
Cherry
Cherry (sour)
Cherry compote
Cherry juice
Clementine
Clementines
Compote (fruits of the season)
Currant juice (black)
Currants (black)
Currants (red)
Dates dried
Dates red
Fig
Fig dried
Gail plum
Ginkgo fruit
Grape juice red
Grape juice white
Grapefruit (Pomelo)
Grapefruit juice
Grapes red
Grapes white
Greengage
Kaki plum
Kiwi

Lime
Luo Han Guo fruit
Lychee
Lychee in Preserved
Mango
Mango juice
Medlar
Mirabelle plum
Mulberry fruit
Nectarine
Orange
Orange dried peel
Orange jam
Orange juice
Papaya
Passion fruit
Peaches
Peaches (canned)
Pear
Pear juice
Pineapple
Pineapple (from a can)
Pineapple juice without sugar
Plum
Plum dried
Plums
Pomegranate
Prickly pear
Quince
Raisins
Red berry (without sugar)
Rose hip
Sour cherries
Strawberries
Strawberry jam
Strawberry Juice
Sugar fructose - fruit sugar
Sugar glucose - grapes sugar
Supplementary nutrition
Tangerine
Watermelon

11 Herbs and their effects

11.1 Basil

It has a beneficial effect on flatulence and nausea, relaxing and soothing. Good to fight emphysema, bronchitis, whooping cough, high blood pressure, headache, mouth odor, warts, hiccup, gout, migraine.

11.2 Mugwort

Reduces bleeding, alleviates pain. In the kitchen, mugwort is used as a spice for fat food. Since it contains many bitter substances, it boosts fat burning and promotes digestion.

11.3 Savory

Stomach-strengthening, soothing and appetizing. Ideal for prevent colds, strengthens the immune system. In case of incontinence or nocturnal wetting (not for children), put the beans in liquor for libido.

11.4 Nettles

Promotes urination. Tea or juice, cleanses the blood and the kidneys, supports prostate problems, inhibit the formation of inflammation, pain-relieving.

11.5 Dill

The medicinal and spice herb has an antispasmodic effect and stimulates gastric juice production. Good to fight flatulence. Antispasmodic for gastrointestinal discomfort.

11.6 Chamomile

Antispasmodic and anti-inflammatory for digestive disorders, soothes the nerves and promotes good sleep. Applied externally, it heals wounds in the mouth-throat area and the skin. Strengthens eyesight.

11.7 Chervil dried

Forces urination, detoxifying, blood-purifying and blood-pressure-reducing effects.

11.8 Coriander

The essential oils are appetizing, digestive, cramping and soothing in stomach and intestinal disorders.

11.9 Coriander (fresh)

The essential oils are appetizing, digestive, cramping and soothing in stomach and intestinal disorders.

11.10   Herbs various

Appetizing, lots of trace elements and vitamins

11.11   Cress

Diuretic, supports urination. Good to fight dry mouth, inner agitation, sore throat, diabetes, kidney stones, gastrointestinal complaints, lung problems, menstrual cramps or cancer.

11.12   Chives

Bactericide, prevents cancer, strengthens gastric juice production, promotes digestion and blood circulation, promotes growth, triggers stagnation.

11.13   Lovage

Stimulates digestion, reduces pain. Extracts of the root are used to flush out urinary tract infections and prevent kidney gravel.

11.14   Lily bulbs

Calms nerves, good to fight scaly skin. The onions and the petals are added to ointments in the Orient, which can heal muscles and tendons. White lily (astringent).

11.15   Dandelion (young plants)

Detoxifies, relieves inflammation. Regulates digestion, helps with rheumatism, releases kidney stones, leaves pimples and chronic skin disorders disappear.

11.16 Marjoram

Helps to digest fat foods, strengthens digestive organs, helps to fight colds, strengthens menstruation, promotes skin healing.

11.17 Oregano fresh

It has an anti-digestive, calming and nerve-strengthening effect, helps to fight cramping stomach and intestinal disorders. The ingredient Carvacrol has an anti-inflammatory effect.

11.18 Oregano dried

It has an anti-digestive, calming and nerve-strengthening effect, helps to fight cramping stomach and intestinal disorders. The ingredient Carvacrol has an anti-inflammatory effect.

11.19 Parsley

Stimulates liver function, detoxifies. Forces urinating. Relieves flatulence. Digestive and menstrual stimulating, birth-accelerating, memory-enhancing, blood-purifying, skin-smoothing.

11.20 Peppermint

Relaxes, frees the lungs and the nose (inhale), regulates the cycle. Stimulates bile flow and bile production, antispasmodic in gastrointestinal disorders, antimicrobial and antiviral.

11.21 Rosemary

Promotes digestion, relieves bloating, strengthens lung, spleen and kidney. Affects the circulation and nerves. Appetizing. Baths help to fight circulatory disorders as well as with gout and rheumatism.

11.22 Sage

Good to fight yeast infections. The leaves have a digestive effect and are used in greasy foods. Antiperspirant effect. Helps to relieve coughing attacks. Dries out (TCM).

11.23 Sorrel

Astringent, hematopoietic, purifies the blood, diuretic. Good to fight liver weakness, upset stomach, indigestion, constipation, diarrhea, worms, scurvy, anemia, women's complaints, wounds, skin rashes, boils, ulcers, swelling.

11.24   Black caraway

Detoxifying, immunoregulatory. In addition, the oil should stimulate the formation of bone marrow cells and generally protect body cells from viruses.

11.25   Thyme dried

Disinfecting. It stimulates the blood circulation, increases the appetite and helps to digest fat meat better. Strengthens lungs and spleen (TCM).

11.26   King Solomon's-seal

Used to repair wounds or damaged tissue. Good to fight dry cough, earlier also tuberculosis and dysentery, as well as diarrhea and hemorrhoids.

11.27   Yam root, yam root tuber

Solves cramps (in the gastrointestinal tract). Digestive through increased bile production. Anti-inflammatory in rheumatic diseases.
Mucolytic agent for coughing. Relief of menopausal symptoms.

12 Basics of Nutrition

The basic principles of nutrition described herein are general recommendations. They are not aimed at a specific form of therapy. Recommendations concerning a therapy have priority.

12.1 Nutrition

Regular meals in a relaxed atmosphere. A warm breakfast is considered a good start into the day.
The main meals ought to be taken for lunch – supper in the early evening. Pay attention to feeling hungry or sated: don't eat too much nor remain hungry is the rule
Prepare the meals freshly from natural, regional products. Frozen, heat-conserved, industrially prepared or foodstuffs cooked in the microwave oven are rejected.
Choice of foodstuffs according to the season: more cooling food in summer, more warming food in winter.
Eat cooked food at least twice a day. Food and drinks ought to be lukewarm, never ice-cold or hot.
Raw vegetables, briefly cooked vegetables, freshly squeezed juices and mineral water are not recommended. Milk and dairy products are only included in the diet if they don't cause problems.
Don't use therapeutic recipes over a longer period without consulting your doctor or therapist.

Varied food
Enjoy the diversity of foodstuffs. Characteristics of a balanced nutrition are variety, suitable combination and a balanced quantity of rich and low energy foodstuffs (on one hand avoiding undersupply with essential nutrients and on the other hand to take to many undesirable substances).

A lot of Cereal Products - and Potatoes
Bread, pasta, rice, cereal flakes (best wholemeal) as well as potatoes contain almost no fat, but many vitamins, mineral nutrients, trace elements, roughage and secondary plant substances. These foodstuffs ought to be taken with low-fat side dishes.

Vegetables and Fruit – „Take Five" every day ...
5 portions of vegetables and fruit a day, as fresh as possible, briefly cooked, or maybe one portion as a juice – ideal as a side dish to every meal as well as snack between meals: Thus a lot of vitamins, mineral nutrients as well as roughage and secondary plant substances

Daily milk and dairy products
Milk and Dairy Products every Day, once or twice per Week Fish;
meat, sausages as well as eggs moderately. These foodstuffs contain
valuable nutrients like calcium in the milk, iodine selenium and omega-3
fat acids in saltwater fish. Meat is favorable due to its high content of
disposable iron and the vitamins B1, B6 and B12. Quantities of 300 – 600
g meat and sausage per week are sufficient. Prefer low-fat products,
especially in meat- and dairy products.

Low-fat and fatty Foodstuffs
Fat supplies us with essential fat acids and fatty foodstuffs contain also
fat-soluble vitamins. Fat is high in energy; therefore much fat in the food
may cause overweight, possibly also cancer. Too many saturated fat
acids may further a tendency for cardio-vascular diseases in the long
term. Prefer vegetable oils and fats (e.g. rapeseed-, olive-, soya-oils and
solid fats produced therefrom). Beware of invisible fat in meat- and dairy
products, pastry and sweets as well as in fast-food and convenience
foods. 70 – 90 g fat per day is sufficient.

Moderately Sugar and Salt
Take sugar and foods/drinks containing various kinds of sugar (e.g.
glucose syrup) only occasionally. Use herbs and spices as well as a little
salt creatively. Prefer salt containing iodine.

Plenty of Liquids
Water is absolutely essential. Drink 1-2 l liquids every day. Prefer water
(with or without gas) and other low-calorie drinks. Alcoholic drinks should
not be taken.

Tasty Dishes, carefully cooked
Cook the meals with as low temperatures and as short as possible, using
little water and fat – this preserves the original taste, keeps the nutrients
intact and prevents the production of harmful compounds.

Take time and enjoy the food
Take your Time and enjoy your Food
Eating consciously helps to eat right. The eye enjoys food, too. It's fun,
invites to enjoy varied dishes and stimulates the feeling of satiety.

Watch your Weight and stay in Motion
A balanced diet and a lot of exercise and sport (30 – 60 min/day) are a
healthy combination. The right weight furthers well-being and health.
Thermals, directional effectiveness, digestive power

There are various criteria for judging the effectiveness of herbs and foodstuffs.

The use of certain herbs and ingredients is based on observations of the effects on the body which these foodstuffs, herbs and spices show after having eaten them. The medical science has developed following system: Every ingredient or herb has a directional effectiveness. Furthermore, there are herbs which have a special effect on certain organs.

The basic condition for a healthy metabolism is to obtain sufficient energy from food and that the digestive process doesn't use too much energy. An easily digestible meal makes content and sated, doesn't cause flatulence and fatigue after the meal. The perfect spices increase the healthiness of our meals. Very often, just small doses of herbs and spices will suffice. They are not used to make us sated, but to help our digestive organs to digest the food.

12.2 Recipes

The recipes list the ingredients to be used and the cooking instructions show how the dish is prepared. The list of ingredients shows the concerned quantities as well as the relevance for the therapy. If you find „less than mentioned", try to comply or find an alternative from the „list of recommended foodstuffs". Mostly it shall result just in a small change of taste when you simply avoid this ingredient.

Mild cooking methods: boiling, stewing, poaching, steaming
Strong cooking methods: barbecuing, roasting, frying, smoking
Balanced cooking methods: deep-frying, baking brick
Deep-freezing and warming in the microwave oven should be avoided (denaturalization).

12.3 Foodstuffs

Foodstuffs have an effect on body and soul like medicinal herbs, only a very much milder one. Dietary advice is mainly based on regional foodstuffs. The knowledge about the effects of each foodstuff and the knowledge, when which foodstuff shall be used, is based on the orthodoschool of medicine. Use ecologic-organic products, if possible. As everything should be cooked for a long time due to a better digestability and very rarely eaten raw, the food agrees with everyone.

The classification of the foodstuffs according to their effect on the body is the basis in order to achieve a harmonious status of health.

Dietary advisors do not recommend certain foodstuffs for everyone. The individual diet is tailor-made for the individual constitution.

Buy only fresh and ripe fruit and vegetables. You ought to leave unripe fruit and vegetables and such with brown spots and wilted leaves behind in the market. In this case take deep-frozen goods (never ready-to-serve dishes!). Fruit and vegetables are deep-frozen immediately after harvesting and often contain more vitamins and minerals than the goods from the vegetable shelf. Whereas conserved or tinned goods contain very much less biological substances. Also, salt, sugar and others are mostly added to the latter. Never leave the foodstuffs in the water after washing them to avoid that many vital substances get drowned. Clean salads, fruit and vegetables immediately before serving.

Please make sure of the hygienic processing of foodstuffs. Clean your salads, fruit and vegetables carefully. When cooking with meat, prepare all ingredients first and then process the meat products. Clean the worktop and tools very carefully. Wooden surfaces ought to be treated with a mild disinfectant regularly in order to reduce germination.

Store fruit and vegetables separately, if possible. Harvested fruit and vegetables are still alive and emit e.g. ethylene gas, which makes other products ripen and age faster. Keep meat and fish in the closed packaging or store them in the fridge in closed containers.

12.4 Herbs

There are some basic rules for storing medicinal herbs. On principle, herbs must be protected from direct sunlight, humidity and heat.

Containers for the storage of herbs may be glasses, ceramic jars and even plastic containers. However, plastic is a rather unsuitable material and should only be a short-term solution. In case of glass containers, use a dark material.

Medicinal herbs cannot be kept for any long period. The shelf life of herbs is limited. However, it can be prolonged with suitable storage. The place should be dark, rather cool and absolutely dry. A wooden medicine cabinet, placed not directly next to a source of heat, would be ideal. Never buy large quantities of herbs so as not to have to throw them away. Label the container with the name of the herb and the date of harvesting or processing.

13 Other dietic-books

The following syndromes of dietetics, TCM or for a therapy supplement for cancer are available.

Dietetics

E001. Nutrition of the infant - baby food
E002. Nutrition during lactation
E003. Nutrition in old age
E004. Nutrition of children and adolescents
E005. Nutrition of athletes
E006. Light weight
E007. Pregnancy
E008. Full food

Protein and electrolyte - kidneys
E009. (hemodialysis) dialysis treatment
E010. Acute renal failure
E011. Chronic renal insufficiency
E012. Nephrotic syndrome
E013. Kidney stones (nephrolithiasis)

Gastrointestinal tract - pancreas
E014. Acute pancreatitis (inflammation of the pancreas)
E015. Chronic pancreatitis (inflammation of the pancreas)

Gastrointestinal tract - small intestine and large intestine
E016. Acute obstipation (constipation)
E017. Chronic obstipation (constipation)
E018. Colon irritabile
E019. Diverticulitis
E020. Acquired lactose intolerance (lactose malabsorption)
E021. Fructose malabsorption
E022. Glutensensitive enteropathy (celiac disease)
E023. Colectomy
E024. Short Bowel Syndrome

Gastrointestinal tract - liver, gallbladder, bile ducts
E025. Acute and chronic hepatitis (inflammation of the liver)
E026. Cholelithiasis (bile stones)
E027. fatty liver
E028. cirrhosis

Gastrointestinal tract - Stomach and duodenal intestine
E029. Acute gastritis
E030. Chronic gastritis
E031. Stomach bleeding
E032. Ulcus ventriculi and duodenal ulcer
E033. Condition after gastric surgery

Gastrointestinal tract - oral cavity and esophagus
E034. Stomatitis
E035. Esophageal carcinoma (esophageal cancer)
E036. Refluosophagitis (heartburn)

Special diseases
E037. Phenylketonuria (PKU)
E038. Rheumatic joint diseases

Metabolism
E039. Obesity (overweight)
E040. Diabetes mellitus
E041. Eating disorders (underweight)

Fat metabolism
E042. Hypercholesterolaemia (increased cholesterol level)
E043. Hepatic Encephalopathy

Heart and circulation
E044. Arteriosclerosis (arterial calcification)
E045. Heart insufficiency
E046. Hypertension
E047. Hyperuricaemia and gout

Changed nutrient requirements
E048. In case of fever
E049. For malignant diseases
E050. After burns
E051. Radiation and chemotherapy

CANCER
E100. Pancreatic cancer
E101. Bladder cancer
E102. Blood cancer (leukemia)
E103. Breast cancer
E104. Colorectal cancer
E105. Gastric cancer
E106. Kidney cancer
E107. Esophageal cancer

TCM
E200. Bladder - moisture heat in the bladder
E201. Bladder - moisture and cold in the bladder
E202. Bladder - emptiness and cold in the bladder
E203. Large intestine - external cold affects the large intestine
E204. Large intestine - moisture heat in the large intestine
E205. Large intestine - heat blocks the intestine II acute
E206. Large intestine - dryness of the colon
E207. Large intestine - Yang deficiency (cold)
E208. Heart - Blood insufficiency
E209. Heart - Blood stagnation
E210. Heart - Fire
E211. Heart - Hot mucus clogs the heart pores

E212. Heart - Cold mucus clogs the heart pores
E213. Heart - Qi deficiency
E214. Heart - Yang deficiency
E215. Heart - Yin deficiency
E216. Liver - Ascending Liver Yang
E217. Liver - Blood deficiency
E218. Liver - Blood stagnation
E219. Liver - Moisture heat in liver and gall bladder
E220. Liver - Fire
E221. Liver - Gall bladder Qi-Empty
E222. Liver - Cold in the liver meridian
E223. Liver - Qi stagnation
E224. Liver - Wind
E225. Liver - Wind with ascending liver Yang
E226. Liver - Wind with blood anemic
E227. Liver - Wind with extreme heat
E228. Lung - Qi deficiency
E229. Lung - Mucus-moisture in the lungs
E230. Lung - Mucus-heat in the lungs
E231. Lung - Mucus-cold in the lungs
E232. Lung - Dryness of the lungs
E233. Lung - Wind-heat attacks the lungs
E234. Lung - Wind-cold affects the lungs
E235. Lung - Yin deficiency
E236. Stomach - Bloodstagnation
E237. Stomach - Fire
E238. Stomach - Cold with liquid
E239. Stomach - Nutrition stagnation
E240. Stomach - Qi deficiency
E241. Stomach - Rebellious Qi
E242. Stomach - Yin Emptiness
E243. Spleen - Heat and moisture attack the spleen
E244. Spleen - Coldness and moisture affects the spleen
E245. Spleen - Qi deficiency
E246. Spleen - Qi deficiency + Declining spleen Qi
E247. Spleen - Qi deficiency + spleen does not control the blood
E248. Spleen - Yang deficiency
E249. Kidney - Heart and kidney no longer communicate
E250. Kidney - Jing deficiency
E251. Kidney - Kidneys cannot receive the Qi
E252. Kidney - Qi is not stable
E253. Kidney - Yang deficiency
E254. Kidney - Yin deficiency

For further information visit di-book.com.